Also by Kingsley Joblin

Getting There is Half the Fun

Reader, I Married Them

Sacred Books of the World and Their Message for Our Time

Servant to First Nations

A Biography of Elgie Joblin

Servant to First Nations

A Biography of Elgie Joblin

Kingsley Joblin

Northern Spirit Publications

Published by Northern Spirit Publications/Workplace Wisdom
a division of Superior Medical Limited
520 Champagne Drive, Downsview, Ontario, Canada M3J 2T9

Graphic Design & Editorial Layout: Diego D'Amario

Printed in the United States of America

National Library of Canada Cataloguing in Publication Data

Joblin, Kingsley, 1912 -
Servant to first nations : a biography of Elgie Joblin

ISBN 0-9688116-4-7

1. Joblin, Elgie E. M. (Elgie Ellingham Miller), 1909 -
2. Indians of North America—Missions—Ontario—History—20th century.
3. United Church of Canada—Missions—Ontario—History—20th century.
4. Missionaries—Ontario—Biography.
5. United Church of Canada—Clergy—Biography.
I. Title.

BX9883.J618J62 2002 266'.792'092 C2002-901247-3

To Dorothy:
a caring sister

Elgie Ellingham Miller Joblin

Foreword

"To every action there is an equal and opposite reaction." Whether or not it is universally true, this formula has been amply demonstrated in recent evaluations of the work of Christian missionaries among the native peoples of Canada. Once universally admired not only as apostles of the faith but as benefactors of the people among whom they worked, they are now generally condemned as ignorant and even pernicious meddlers with cultures they took no trouble to understand. A more nuanced appraisal is needed, and even a defence of their work, before we can recognize that the enterprise had its benefits and even its heroes and heroines.

Kingsley Joblin, whose brother Elgie was actively and indeed prominently engaged in it, views many of its aspects in a more favourable light. As we read on, we shall see that Elgie was by no means unaware of some of the shadows of the Christian approach to the Indians and actually devoted the greater part of his life to lightening them. Kingsley Joblin, as all who know him will be aware, is both a competent scholar and a born raconteur. Reading his book, therefore, will both enlighten and entertain.

I am sure that you will be impressed, as I was, by the depth of Elgie Joblin's vision of what can be done for the native peoples. He did much for them himself, but also inspired them by his conviction of what they can do for themselves if not hindered by an over-zealous bureaucracy that knows exactly what is good for them. I commend this book to anyone who is concerned for the future of an increasingly large component of the Canadian population and especially to those who are in positions that will have a special bearing on their future. For those in positions of authority or influence in the United Church of Canada it is essential reading.

My only significant contact with Elgie Joblin was at a conference of the Lorrain Fellowship on the shore of Lake Timiskaming in 1964 (pp. 117-121). We were both speakers at it, although he was undoubtedly the star. Not only his intimate knowledge of the first people and their problems but also his obvious delight in his contacts with them were abundantly evident. His enthusiasm and insight were a major factor in stimulating my interest in learning more about the subject. I hope that nothing I have written will seem to him too insensitive. Knowing his insistence on having an encyclopedic knowledge of "things Indian," I am certain that he will have been familiar with it.

John Webster Grant

Contents

Preface

It will soon become obvious to a reader that I refer to our first citizens of Canada as "Indians," not as aborigines or First Nations, the terms now in use. It was as Indians that they were known throughout the period covered in this biography, in governmental and church records, and in common speech. I hope my respected fellow citizens take no offence at this. It would have been anachronistic to do otherwise.

In the second place, the language used is informal. The writer often uses the first person when referring to his relationship with the main character. And he is always "Elgie," not Mr. or Dr. Joblin. Though I was three years his junior, we were close to each other until our long period of education was over and our paths separated. Even then we kept in touch.

Stories from the early years, therefore, derive from personal reminiscences. Subsequent material is based on his carefully kept records, most of which are to be found in the United Church archives, and in his journal, which reflects on his busy life and deals with its personal aspects. No doubt a member of the family is unlikely to write an objective biography. But it may well be that some historian in the new millennium, writing when there has been a happy outcome to two centuries of trial and error in the treatment and education of Canada's aborigines, may find these pages useful in tracking how the outcome emerged.

The table of contents is arranged on the analogy of a symphony. Elgie Joblin loved music, but his life gave him little opportunity to attend concerts. He had to be content with his record collection. I see his life as a symphony, with a dominant *motif* from beginning to end.

I am indebted to my daughter Dale who deciphered my handwriting and transcribed it on that mysterious machine known as a word processor. I am also grateful to the historian John Webster Grant (author of *The Moon of Wintertime*, U.C.P.H. Press, among many scholarly books), for his Foreword.

Kingsley Joblin

Fanfare

A Symphony in Words

Most biographies are of people well known to the public. No reason need be given for writing, and there is a ready-made audience. The subject of this book is in a different situation. Elgie Joblin believed that it was the work that was important, not the worker, and he loved his work. He kept careful records so that its importance might be recognized, its achievement maintained, and its lessons of failure and success valued by those who followed him. His focus was on the aborigines who were his friends and his primary concern.

While most biographies end with tributes to the famous subject who has been portrayed, this one begins with them. They are placed first to assure the reader that this little-known person is worthy of their interest. Here are some of them.

When he retired in 1970 as associate secretary of the Board of Home Missions of the United Church of Canada, the minutes refer to "the warm charm of his personality and the ringing challenge of his faith and hope and courage." Then they go on to say:

> The report on the Indian work in 1969 is a finished product. Elgie may have begun his connection with the Indian work in 1932 as a student minister with everything to learn about the Indian people, but though he moved through the intermediate steps as teacher and principal who could teach them, it is obvious from his report that he is one of the men who has helped to build the "two-way bridge" of which he speaks.
>
> He feels himself privileged, and reminds us that we are obligated as well as privileged to share in the Indians' struggle for life, self-determination, and dignity. Had the Government of Canada learned something of his humility and dedication in dealing with the native peoples, the climate today might have been more conducive

> to understanding and brotherhood—perhaps it will be yet.
>
> The report reveals an amazing grasp of a multitude of the details of the work, but more important still, a knowledge of the people, both those served and those serving them.
>
> When he says to his fellow-workers that "the Board is fortunate indeed to have the services of such able and dedicated men," we reach back into history for the response "Et tu!", you too, Elgie. The Board and the Indian people say, "Thank you, God, for Elgie!"

To see how far back Elgie had been working to change "the climate" of which the Minutes speak, consider these words from historian John Webster Grant's *The Moon of Wintertime*, p. 206:

> Although church leaders were taken aback by the sudden onslaught of criticism, they were not altogether unprepared to respond to it creatively . . . In 1944 E. E. M. Joblin of the United Church urged "working with, not for, Indians." In 1947 a United Church delegation (of which he was a member) to a special parliamentary committee called for the abolition of wardship and far more self-government on Reserves.

Elgie submitted his resignation as supervisory principal at Muncey after twenty-one years of service to the Indians there. This had made possible his appointment to the board that gave the tribute just mentioned, though he did not know it at the time. His resignation also elicited a letter from the superintendent of schools to the Indian Affairs branch in Ottawa. We will quote it more fully later, but it begins: "Undoubtedly you were disturbed, as I surely was, to receive a resignation from Mr. Joblin." It then lists his accomplishments and goes on to say, "In view of these circumstances it would be very regrettable if Mr. Joblin should be allowed to pass out of the picture." The superintendent then suggests that he be posted to London, and from there supervise all the Indian schools in southwest Ontario. Before that could happen, Elgie was persuaded by the Board of Home Missions of the United Church to supervise their work with Indians across Canada.

When he resigned from *that* work after fourteen busy years there was a flood of letters of appreciation from his wide-ranging constituency. Elgie's helpfulness had done much to sustain the workers in the field. The words of Ray Smith in Manitoba are representative of their thankful response:

> You have heard many words of appreciation for your outstanding service to the Church, and this is one more. Here in Manitoba we have felt the full impact of your concern and leadership as you have shown the capacity to bridge the gap between the native Canadians and the white majority. I am sure that time will reveal the greatness of your leadership and the enduring qualities of your Christian concern . . .

The Indians themselves were represented by Chief Judge Nelles Buchanan, whom Elgie had persuaded to sit on the Board of Home Missions representing Alberta:

> I am quite loath to have you depart from the service of the Board, and I don't think your share in its load calls for a younger person. In any event, I again express to you my appreciation for the contribution you have made to my own life. The materials that have come from your pen have been most helpful . . .

Even the government of Canada could join this chorus. For those fourteen years he had attended meetings of the Indian Affairs Branch in Ottawa. In 1969 a young minister of Indian Affairs and Northern Development, Jean Chrétien, introduced a new policy to the House that would give the Indians much more independence. Elgie obtained a copy and asked the executive of the board to study it with him, and authorize him to write his comments to Mr. Chrétien. The intent of the bill and the correspondence will be discussed later, but here I quote from the minister's letter:

Dear Reverend Joblin,

I appreciated this letter more than I can say. Of all those I have received since these policy proposals were first put forward, it shows the most careful thought and deepest understanding of what the Government is proposing for the Indian people of Canada. I appreciated your cogent and perceptive remarks which also reveal your awareness of the difficulties to be faced if these proposals are to be translated into reality . . . Your influence will be of enormous assistance in encouraging the Indian people in their search for equality, self determination, and responsibility. Thank you again.

Yours sincerely, Jean Chrétien

The historian Peter S. Schmalz discusses Indian education in his book, *The Ojibwa of Northern Ontario* (University of Toronto Press, Toronto, 1991, p. 191) and pays this tribute to Elgie almost in passing:

> The only source of qualified white teachers were the provincial Normal Schools. In 1947 Elgie Joblin, in his analysis of Indian education, recognized some of the deficiencies in teacher training, and suggested modest improvements. In addition to in-service training, he recommended that some attention be given educational psychology, kindergarten-primary methods, and the aims and objectives of the coming school year. What was considered most innovative was his suggestion that classes be held on "the historical background of the Indian people." This was the first time that an educator had proposed that teachers should learn something of the heritage of the people they had been trying to instruct for over one hundred years.

To finish this introduction with a Latin flourish, here is the end of the testimonial presenting Elgie to convocation when he was given a Doctor of Divinity degree:

> Quibus de causis, praeclarissime cancellari, praesento tibi Elgie Ellingham Miller Joblin, postulans ut eum admittas in gradum doctoris in divinitate, honoris causa.

First Movement

Theme One: The Early Years

II Parentage

It is said that when a tourist asked the way to Dublin, an Irishman replied, "If I were going to Dublin, sure and I wouldn't start from here!" One might have said the same about Elgie. He was born while his father was the village schoolteacher in Castleton, Ontario. His date of birth was April 6th, 1909. Perhaps someone adept in the pseudo-science of astrology could say whether or not the date was an auspicious one. I would reply that the credit for his journey from Castleton to the committee rooms of Ottawa and the head office of the United Church in Toronto goes not to his stars but to his character, shaped through what others might regard as a journey that was uphill much of the way.

There is no doubt that one of the stars that guided him was his father, so we should know something about Frederick George Joblin. Like his son after him, his career alternated between teaching and ministry. He received a teaching certificate from the Whitby "Model School" in 1898. No teaching job was available, so after working in a Toronto hardware store in the spring, he went West on one of the "Harvesters Specials" to work on a Manitoba farm. In the fall, on the strength of his former leadership in Sunday school and youth groups in Simcoe Street Methodist Church, Oshawa, he was appointed to minister to Foxton Mission, near Teulon in rural Manitoba. As he said later, they were hard up for ministers on the Prairies.

At last in 1900 he secured work for which he felt better trained. For three years he oversaw a one-room log schoolhouse at Leeburn Ontario, seventeen miles from Bruce Mines in Algoma. Forty years later I took him there on the way to Sault Ste. Marie and was astonished at the warmth of his welcome in the homes of former students who were now grandparents.

Feeling the need to upgrade his teaching certificate, he went to Toronto Normal School in 1903. While attending Clinton Street Methodist Church he met Flora Elgie. This is the source of Elgie's unusual Christian name. (The poor child was also saddled with the surnames of the maternal grandparents on both sides—Ellingham Miller.

He bore the burden bravely, aware that he was the first grandson in both families.) Soon a voluminous correspondence began, because Fred was appointed in 1904 as missionary teacher at Norway House and then at Cross Lake, Northern Manitoba. This continued for two years. Mail service was sporadic, so the letters were written on onion skin, a thin, almost transparent paper. Not only that; when a page was covered, it was turned sideways and written across (yes, it *is* possible to read such a letter. No doubt the eyes of love helped).

After this strenuous stint, Fred Joblin was appointed missionary-teacher to the Alderville Reserve near Rice Lake, Ontario, and a year later brought his bride to the teacherage there. After the wedding at the home of the bride, 21 Havelock Street in Toronto, there followed an unusual honeymoon trip. The train took the happy couple to Cobourg, where they were met by the chief with a "democrat," now called a buckboard, and driven to Alderville. Incidentally, there was neither indoor plumbing nor electricity to ease the city-bred bride into her new calling. And never again until retirement in Port Perry was she to know the luxury of a bathroom.

After the birth of Gladys May in 1907 it was evident that improvements in accommodation and salary were needed. Fred became the teacher in Castleton Village. For three years he not only taught, but studied for the ministry through correspondence with Victoria University in Toronto. He went there for examinations periodically—and did very well indeed according to his records, which are still available. This led to his appointment in 1911 as minister-on-probation at Melrose, a three-point charge near Shannonville. He was ordained to the Methodist ministry in 1912. Since Elgie had been added to the family in 1909, we turn now to his story to discover the father's influence on the son.

III The Early Years

In an old family photograph Elgie is sitting on the ground with other children. His father is in the row immediately behind him, and his hand seems to be resting on Elgie's head. When he came across this in his retirement years, Elgie was pleased at the apparent symbolism: one generation passing on its work and its blessing to another. We shall see how apt this was. Nevertheless, I believe it was from his mother that he inherited his disposition.

Mother was a doer. "Whatsoever your hand finds to do, do it with all your might." If fate had cast her lot in a convent, she would have been its general manager, not a contemplative. I don't think this was because her husband needed a practical hand at the family helm, or that having five children forced her into this role. If a disposition can be inherited, there is evidence of this. Her father was just such a type. Herbert Elgie was a builder. By his hard work, skill, and integrity he rose from humble beginnings to be the president of the Toronto Board of Trade. At the time our story opened, while his friend John Joblin was Bible class leader and choirmaster in Clinton Street Methodist Church, Herbert Elgie was a church steward and was soon to build (and largely finance) a new church.

In his practical ability and his need to be *doing* something, Elgie followed this tradition. My earliest memory of him is typical. He could have been no more than seven, but he was raking the leaves in the parsonage yard at Bayside and had started a fire to burn them. My little sister Dorothy and I had clambered into the wheelbarrow beside the fire and were dancing there happily when it capsized us into the fire. I rolled clear; my sister didn't, and received a severe burn to her arm. Her cries brought Elgie running to the rescue, and he carried or perhaps dragged her into the house where Mother administered the all-purpose salve Mecca. I am tempted to point out that he was working while I danced.

"One swallow does not make a summer." But there are many more of the same flock. Dad had been a popular minister in the Bayside area, between Belleville and Trenton. He was asked to return there from his pastorate in Seagrave to be principal of the two-roomed school and to persuade the farmers to vote for the establishment of a continuation school. This would provide further education for the graduates of the "entrance class" (Grade 8). Elgie was about eleven, but he got a job at the cheese factory after school and on Saturdays across the "Kingston Highway" from the teacherage. He would tell us when the curd was being cut, and we younger siblings would appear for a handout. In the holidays he found other jobs. I remember him helping shingle a shed roof—at age 12! Then a group of us were recruited to pick peas at so much a basket. Having set us to work, the farmer left. It was a hot July day. The Bay of Quinte sparkled not far away. By midafternoon all of us bolted for a swim, leaving only Elgie and the farmer's son to slave on. The farmer returned before we did. In his righteous anger he paid us nothing. Our lack of virtue was suitably rewarded.

"The boy is father to the man." In this story we are going to be dealing with a remarkable man. What shaped that character? The old argument continues on the relative importance of heredity and environment. I have just been telling of Elgie's frequent choice of work over play. Could he have inherited a gene that would encourage such choices? Or had the Protestant work ethic already been instilled?

It seems not, since the boy actually enjoyed working. That, at least, was my observation as I grew up beside him. Thanks to Mother's organizational genius, each one of her five children had a specific list of chores to do, after which our time was our own. I remember some satisfaction in seeing that the woodboxes were filled; but my real desire was to arrive at playtime. The action itself seemed rewarding to my brother.

I'm not saying that he did not thoroughly enjoy play. At that time Robin Hood was in vogue. What bows we made! What arrows, whittled from light driftwood found on the shores of Quinte. What skill he achieved in target practice. One of my chores was to bring home the two-quart honey-pail of milk from the neighbouring farm. As I approached, I set it on a stump and challenged him to hit it. He did, with the first arrow. But there was no milk that day.

In lieu of an adequate salary, the teacher was provided with two acres of garden land from which to provide his family's sustenance. Dad laboured hard before and after school to see that it was all planted. All the space not devoted to vegetables was planted with winter beans, those hard little white ones—so nourishing, so . . . One of W. B. Yeats' charming poems has him standing on a city street, longing for a peaceful retreat in the country. "Nine bean rows will I have there . . ." But suppose he had had ninety?

My brother and I had the job of hoeing those beans, one of us on each side of the row. How well I recall the drudgery. "I like hoeing beans," said this annoying brother.

I have been making the case that Elgie inherited a gene from his mother's side of the family that made him enjoy action, whether in work or play. I should now like to show the influence of environment in shaping character; and, specifically, the influence of religious faith and custom. In "The Cotter's Saturday Night," Robert Burns extols the influence of the regular family gathering whose climax was reading from the Bible and prayer led by the father. In our home there were readings and prayers seven days a week; then Sunday school and church on Sunday. On that welcome "day of rest" one might read edifying things like Hurlburt's *Story of the Bible* or the Sunday school papers, or go for a quiet walk. No homework was to be done. (For years I enjoyed this tradition in good conscience while my friends toiled at theirs.) The evening ended with singing around the piano. No secular music, please; hymns only, or rousers from the green *New Canadian Hymnal.*

A few years ago there was a discussion in the United Church of Canada about "rites of passage": baptism, confirmation, and so on. It was decided that if at baptism a child is admitted to "the family and household of God," he/she should be welcome to the Table of the Lord, Holy Communion, as part of that family. It had long been the custom, however, to admit to that privilege those of more mature years who had undergone a period of study (the old catechumen class) and had been confirmed in the faith by accepting for themselves the vows undertaken on their behalf in baptism. In the old days in the pre-Union Methodist Church, even this would hardly qualify one. An emotional experience, preferably one that included the conviction of sin and salvation by the grace of Christ and commitment to the way of perfection, was highly valued. Evangelistic rallies or revivals were organized to encourage response to an "altar call."

My brother and I were discussing this issue when he told me of an experience still strong in his memory though it had happened seventy years before, probably in Seagrave where we had moved in 1916. In the words of the Invitation to Holy Communion, "all who loved the Lord Jesus Christ" were invited to come forward and share the Loaf and the Cup. Elgie loved the Lord, and went forward. How heads must have turned! "What is that child doing there?!" I am sure our father was startled. And I am sure it was to his credit that the child was not rebuffed. Of such was the Kingdom.

His commitment was not merely an emotional one. A story from his teen years illustrates his integrity. For years Dad had owned an acetylene projector, and would order slides from the Methodist Book Room for evenings of education and entertainment in rural churches. Elgie mastered the tricky job of keeping the burners just right while inserting the slides, thus leaving Dad free to give the lecture. On one occasion the projector was set up in the balcony of White's Church in Bayside. I was there to keep Elgie company, and perhaps to escape the collection plate on the main floor. After the "show" (this time it was *Ben Hur*), he insisted that we go down and make our contribution. I thought this was carrying scrupulousness a bit too far, though I couldn't have given a name to it.

This story recalls the old teacherage after 1919. It was not idyllic—even with three wood stoves it was cold in the winter. But the worst experience in it was the plague of large sewer rats that came up from the Bay of Quinte and took possession of house and barn. In the barn we trapped them in the oat bin. In the house they multiplied. I remember taking my shoe to what I thought was a mouse, when Mother Rat leaped out at me from a hole under the sink. One night our mother heard the little dog yelping in the kitchen. Lighting a lamp, she went to investigate. About twenty rats had cornered Spot, and he was fighting for his life. Putting down the lamp, she seized a broom and, like Samson of old, "smote them hip and thigh." Then there was the night one attacked Elgie when he was sleeping, biting him severely in a toe. 'Tis true. I shared the bed with him and was a witness.

The toe healed, no doubt with the aid of the ubiquitous Mecca. But another misfortune occurred: scarlet fever. Mother and Elgie were quarantined while the rest of us were sent to Toronto. It was a severe case, and the quarantine lasted eight weeks. Later Elgie said it had at least one good consequence. During convalescence he and Mother grew close together—a nice balance to his former loyalty to Dad. That had been cemented in the Seagrave years, 1914-1918. Elgie had apparently been born with eyes impaired by both astigmatism and short-sightedness. Since he could not see ordinary print, he had been kept home. He learned to read from a large-print *Story of the Bible*. No doubt Dad had also coached him. But the bond was further established as "his father's boy" helped with outside chores: in the garden, bringing in wood as it was split, feeding the horse. It was not until he was nine that Mother took him to a specialist in Toronto. Dr. Colin Campbell was to become the family ophthalmologist for thirty years. With glasses Elgie was able to start school at Grade VI. He would later say that in that one-room school he absorbed what all the grades were doing through osmosis. I know what he meant. I started school the same year at age six. The teacher would have each grade stand in turn in front of her desk while she asked questions. I paid more attention to *them* than to the work I was supposed to be doing at my seat.

Theme Two: Preparation

IV Stirling and the Farm

The problem of eyesight did not seem obvious during his high school years. He was a good listener and quick learner. His older sister claimed to be annoyed when she worked longer and harder than he and got no higher grades. They started high school together while in Bayside, driving the six miles to Trenton and back each day now that Dad's horse was no longer needed for pastoral work. The trips during severe weather in an open cutter must have been uncomfortable, but I never knew them to complain.

When the family moved to Stirling, Ontario, in 1923, high school attendance was easier. It is likely that Dad accepted this Call knowingly and willingly, though it was very demanding. The parsonage, as the manse was called before Church Union, was in the village close to the schools, but the three-point charge called Rawdon was in the surrounding rural area. This required long drives and late returns from evening meetings. His reluctant introduction to the automotive age only came five years later and is the subject of a little book of mine, *Half the Fun.*

Dad loved his rural constituents and could never be enticed to a town pastorate. He believed that his three sons should experience farm life. All of them had a taste of it during school vacations. Elgie enjoyed the taste and stayed for a full meal. He spent two summers on the farm of Gilbert Smith, a fine man and "clerk of session" for the Rawdon charge. As Elgie was finishing his fifth year or Grade XIII, Mr. Smith had a heart attack and begged him to run the farm until his recovery. He enjoyed it all and stayed for two years. The uninitiated may think of farming as a simple life, but the modern farmer must be a talented man to survive. He must not only understand animals, seeds, and seasons; he must be adept at repairing machinery. Elgie found himself in his element, and I remember his satisfaction in repairing the old milking machine that was operated by a one-cylinder gas engine. Then when winter brought spare hours he went to work on the long-defunct Chevrolet 490 touring car and got it running again.

There was another side to this life on the farm: participation in the life of the community. This meant more than playing ball on the local team. In those days the church was the centre around which life revolved. There were one-act plays; there was a Young Peoples' Society that Dad had organized, and for which he provided "carpet balls" in the recreation period. There was a Youth Bible Class which Elgie was persuaded to teach. And there were the church services with enthusiastic choirs. Talk about involvement!

At home in Stirling he had attended the local St. Paul's Church. There had been involvement there too, notably in the Tuxis programme for teenage boys, a church-centred alternative to Boy Scouts. I still remember part of the opening ceremony:

> Life is not a goblet to be drained.
> But a measure to be filled.

It could have been Elgie's motto. He was persuaded to run for the Ontario Older Boys' Parliament, which took place each year in the legislative chamber in Toronto during the Christmas vacation. The campaign took him to various locations in Hastings County. I recall that his opponent was an able—almost flamboyant—speaker. But Elgie's quiet sincerity and well-organized talks won the election. It was his style for fifty years; it was himself.

Sometime during those teen years, he persuaded me to go fifty-fifty with him on the purchase of boxing gloves. A boxer I was not. But he wanted them for recreation time at Tuxis, where they had good workouts. At home he practiced with me. No contest. There was a rule that prohibited blows to the head, but it was hardly necessary; I couldn't get within reach of his glasses. But virtue was rewarded eventually. I inherited those gloves and used them to good effect years later in my summer mission fields.

Another deal was more logical. When he went to work for Gilbert Smith he could no longer attend to the chickens he had brought from Bayside. He sold them to me, and I was a slave to them for three years. In Bayside he had been persuaded to raise pigeons, selling the "squabs," unfledged young birds, to the specialty restaurant trade in Belleville. But he couldn't kill the things, and so he sold the flock to me and went in for chickens. But again virtue was rewarded. The money I made and saved from eggs and the occasional rooster (killed, plucked, and drawn, alas) enabled me to begin my college education.

After this aside about the Stirling years it is time to get back to the influence of Mt. Pleasant Church on the Rawdon charge. Here Elgie was exposed to his father's ministry for two summers and two full years. It is a tribute to that ministry, along with home and church life since his birth, that Elgie felt a compelling call to offer himself to a continuation of that ministry.

It is a good thing when a community not only appreciates one of its own, but shows it. Before he left Mt. Pleasant, his class and the congregation presented him with a fine Omega pocket watch. He cherished it all his life. It is now among my treasures, for it represents a lifetime of service that began so early.

V "On Probation": The Cordova Mines Years

To become a candidate for the ministry one must be recommended by the local church and then by the presbytery. There was no difficulty about that. But where was the money to come from for the required years of arts and theology? There could be no help from Dad's meagre salary. He suggested that Elgie go to Normal School (one year after Grade XIII was sufficient then) and teach in order to save enough. Mother was sure this delay was unnecessary. It was her conviction that if the Lord wills something, the Lord would provide for it. And so the Lord did.

In the old Methodist days, a candidate for the ministry, after due oral examinations, would be given a two-year probation, serving the church under supervision. There was no use wasting money on the education of a dud! It was just three years after Church Union, and the old ways of the three denominations—Congregational, Methodist, and Presbyterian—were allowed to continue during a period of adjustment. Cordova Mines, a three-point charge, was vacant. The iron mines had closed long since, and the villagers and farmers of the area could not afford an ordained minister. The Rev. William Archer of Havelock was willing to supervise. So to Cordova Elgie went, at age nineteen, with no more training than his years within the bosom of the church had given him. At least he could identify with the rural folk he served. And it would be better experience than a year at Normal and another teaching. He felt he was doing what he had been called to do.

One obstacle in his new life—though I doubt if he perceived it as such—was that for the first time he was his own cook and housekeeper. No doubt he would be asked occasionally to stay for a meal on his round of "pastoral visitation." Otherwise he had two reliable standbys: oatmeal for breakfast and beans for the rest. He liked beans. I recall that long before, when Dad was the minister at Seagrave, Elgie would let his six-year-old brother tag along when he went fishing in the local creek. The catch, largely catfish, would be welcome in those almost-meatless World War I days. What would Mother pack for our lunch?

"Just a little lard-pail of beans and two spoons." Little brother did not like beans, but the pail returned empty.

Another obstacle was the draughty old parsonage. The two winters he lived in it were severe, though without sufficient snow to prevent using his Model-T Ford on the rutty roads. Everything seemed normal to him on the February 1930 weekend I visited. He used only the kitchen stove, and since there was no coal, the wood burned out overnight. I was there to preach my first sermon, since I had applied for a summer mission field after one year at college—and I had never prayed in public, let alone preached.

On that Sunday morning I doubted if I could stop my teeth chattering in order to say anything. The water in the kettle on the stove was frozen. This was not unusual, and soon remedied. After our oatmeal we went out to the car to drive to the first church. Too cold for the starter to work; try the crank. It wouldn't budge—no Winter-weight oil in those days. Not unusual. Back into the kitchen to shake the coals down into the ash-holder; out to the car carrying the glowing pan with leather mitts; slide the pan under the engine and wait awhile; try the crank to loosen up the pistons; then use the starter and go. Then at each little church, cover the engine and radiator with an old robe and hope the preacher didn't keep the congregation too long. That day printed my text indelibly on my mind: "They went out to see what was done, and they came to Jesus." At least I had had a taste of how things were done at Cordova Mines.

Looking back on his two years there, Elgie wrote: "At first I had the feeling that I had accomplished very little of real value. Particularly in times of death one feels so helpless. But I found that God was able to use the efforts of even the least effective of us far beyond our deserving." Letters showed that he left behind a grateful people.

VI Victoria College

Having completed his probation at Cordova to the satisfaction of all concerned, in September of 1930 he began his studies toward the B.A. in the arts faculty of Victoria University in the University of Toronto. And here began the only serious disagreement that we ever had—and it was a long-lasting one. He couldn't see the point in "wasting" three years before getting to "the real thing," theology. Perhaps if we had started together, we would have agreed—at least at first. But during the previous years I had completed high school and put in a year at Vic, thanks to a couple of scholarships and the "egg" money. By this time I was completely sold on an arts education. I particularly enjoyed English literature under such luminaries as Profs. Pelham Edgar, John Robins, and E. J. Pratt. When I argued that we needed all the education we could get to preach in today's world, he replied that he had no intention of ministering in towns; he was called to a rural ministry like our father's. He knew the rural mind. What he wanted was bible study and theology, not Shakespeare and philosophy.

Nevertheless, we had two happy years together before I graduated from arts and went west. The first of these was in the old annex to Burwash Hall, Charles House, a big double one at 79/81. He had brought his pride and joy there, a 120-bass piano accordion. Others would drop in after dinner, and we enjoyed some rollicking singsongs, which I accompanied on the violin. (Note that I did not say I played that noble instrument; I worked on it.) On Sundays groups of us went to neighbouring churches, our favourite being Bloor United under Dr. George Pigeon. On Wednesday evenings a group of us "church students" (as candidates for the ministry were called then) went to the parsonage of Dr. E. Cressley Hunter of Carleton United, and listened as he gave generously of his time and experience, answering our questions.

The second year saw the beginning of a family cooperative; perhaps I should say an "extended" family cooperative. Grandma Elgie owned a house on Bedford Road, left to her as a source of income. In exchange for being looked after, she provided lodging there for the following: Elgie and me, providing the food at much less cost than at Burwash Hall; our sister Dorothy, who was at Toronto Normal School; Uncle

Fred Elgie, now a widower and unemployed (1931-32 was deep in the Great Depression); his two little girls, Inez and Margerie; and even, for a while, Uncle Percy Elgie, now estranged from his wife. Our sister Gladys cared for this whole menagerie. Talk about works of supererogation! Except for "the gratifying feeling that her duty had been done" (to quote the Gondoliers), all she got for it was Dorothy's payment for her board once she started teaching. She finally got to Vic herself a year later. But we did have a good time together, especially in our quartet singsongs every night after dinner.

That summer Elgie worked in Stirling helping dig trenches for a new waterworks system. In September he organized another cooperative, this time with several students who could not afford residence fees. It was on Brunswick Avenue, within walking distance of the college. I joined it a year later. Each week we took turns doing the cooking. It was a wonder we survived. Elgie had had his apprenticeship; his favourite was cottage roll—and beans. But the others had had no experience, and we suffered for this lack. I remember coming home to a minor emergency. The week before, Elgie had provided a good rice pudding. Stuart Brown decided to follow suit. He had filled a saucepan with rice and topped it off with water. As it cooked it expanded. Soon every pan we owned was full of half-done rice and none was left to cook anything else. As they say, live and learn. We were young, and we survived.

Before his final year in arts, Elgie applied for, and was given, work that suited him well and pointed the way to his subsequent career, a mission field in Lindsay Presbytery known as the Wesley Charge, named for its largest appointment. Within its boundaries was the Curve Lake Indian Reserve with its United Church. The job involved full-time work for four months in summer, and weekend supply for the rest of the year. This lasted for four years and made him a happy man.

He became so committed to this undertaking that his academic work was neglected. For transportation on the mission he bought an old Plymouth. I remember that when the running boards rusted out he bolted on hardwood planks. During the college season sometimes he skipped Friday (and often Monday) classes. Leaving Thursday afternoon gave him a long (very long) weekend for his "real" calling. At the end of his first year there (and his final one in arts) he wrote his last exam, "Modern History," after a busy week and a full Sunday. He left for Toronto very early Monday morning. The exam was at 9:30. He did not pass. In his journal he makes no excuses, but blames himself for not studying harder. He had learned his lesson and passed the supplemental.

After his arts course we shared classes for three years at Emmanuel Theological College, and he could borrow my notes for classes missed. There was no time for recreation; the essays and examinations filled the hours in Toronto. He did well enough in these. Then came the final year, to which he applied himself with the energy we have come to expect of him. He was able to cut back his ministerial work to every other weekend. He graduated with First-Class Honours and the prize for an "educational" sermon—an interest that was to blossom later through a surprising turn in his career.

He also won the prize in the course on Christian missions. A splendid finale. With the prize money he bought Helen Smith a ring. She deserved it; it had been ten years since their "understanding" when Elgie had worked at the family farm. In the group picture taken after our ordination in 1936 at St. Andrew's United Church, Oshawa, she was there along with our sister Gladys, Father and Mother, and Grandpa and Grandma Joblin. He was ready for a new life with her beside him.

But *we* are not ready to discuss this yet. We must backtrack to those four years as a student minister during his last year in arts and the three in theology. They were to lead to his life work.

There were three churches on the "charge": Wesley, Lakehurst, and the Curve Lake Indian one on the reserve. An isolated one at Blairton had been closed. The people petitioned him to reopen it, which he did, conducting a weeknight service there. The records show that eventually, after confirmation classes, fifteen were received into membership through profession of faith at Lakehurst, eleven at Wesley, and twenty-six at Curve Lake. These figures only hint at his "labours," especially with young people, before they were ready to join such classes and make their commitments. A letter from one of these teenagers, Mrs. Jim Weaver, then Viola Harris, suggests some of "the many ways he endeared himself to the youth of the community. He formed a small band that included my sister and me. It played at social events, not only for the three churches but for neighbouring ones as well. What fun we had! He formed a volleyball team and a baseball team at each church, which brought young people together for tournaments, forming many friendships. He helped our church organist form a youth choir too."

Her letter also speaks of "his beloved cottage on Buckhorn Lake, a haven he shared with many especially us young people whom he loved having around and was, I'm sure, secretly shaping our lives." How could he afford to build a cottage? He bought a long-abandoned log house for $75.00. He hired three unemployed locals to haul the logs and beams to a lot in a pasture owned by the Harris family with whom he boarded. It was rough, "drowned land," flooded by the dam at Buckhorn, full of stumps and shore growth. The lot cost him $100.00. With his brother Fred, who needed a summer job, he raised the logs (carefully marked) into their former position. The old pine flooring could still be used, and the rough-hewn beams for the ceiling. At one corner, there was a sunroom facing the lake. Then came the piece-de-resistance: the fireplace made from local stone (which was everywhere!). For this he employed our Uncle Fred Elgie, also out of a job in those depression years. He was a builder, but his specialty was stonework. To see the beautiful raised "pointing," look at the stone wall surrounding Casa Loma. The pointing is his work, though he had labourers to place the stones. Years ago there was a Book-of-the-Month Club choice entitled *Mr. Blandings Builds His Dream House*. This was Elgie's.

I have observed that twenty-one members had been received into the Curve Lake Indian Church by the end of his ministry there. It was this part of his work that was to shape his future, though it must have been difficult. A report of a visitation committee of Peterborough presbytery is still extant. The members were "shocked" at conditions on the reserve. Most of its fifty-five families lived in "squalor"; there was much alcoholism, illegitimacy, and poverty. The situation in some homes was "unspeakably vile," contrasting with "the minority Christian homes."

There is not a word in his journal about such conditions. Obviously he emphasized the positive in order to eliminate the negative. In his work there he had the enthusiastic support of Chief Dan Whetung, who was postmaster for thirty years and owner of the Whetung Lodge for tourists. The family store has since been remade into an attractive outlet for Indian crafts. Elgie telephoned him one Sunday morning in early spring. The road in had been blocked all winter, so the only access was across the frozen lake. There was water all over the ice. He asked whether it was safe to cross, and the chief said yes. Elgie hoped he was right. Near the shore the water came up to the running boards; he kept the door open in case the car fell through. But the water levelled off to about six inches, and he arrived in time to conduct the service.

"Socials" were popular, and so was the minister with his accordion, who would lead singsongs and organize "pick-up" orchestras. This gave him an idea. There had been no fraternizing between the Indians and the other two congregations. Why not invite the "whites" to a social evening? It took some organizing—and persuasion. The Indians did not think the others would come. But they did. Perhaps there had been some persuading there too! As a result of this happy evening, the officials of the Indian Church were invited to meet with the others in a unified board for the charge.

During the late winter of 1936 there occurred an event that may have determined Elgie's future. This is from his journal:

> Our choir from Curve Lake was invited to sing in one of the Peterborough churches during some kind of missionary presentation. As a part of this, the youngest child of our organist sang a solo. She was about five, and stood on a chair in front of the front seat, where I sat with my accordion, playing only enough to give her a start and a very quiet accompaniment. She and the choir performed very well, and I think some of the credit came my way, much more than I deserved. Dr. Barner, the Supt. of Indian Missions for the whole Church, who had visited twice during my years on the charge, got the idea that I might be a suitable worker among the Indian people.
>
> During the Easter recess I was taken to see something of the work at the Muncey Reserve (between London and Chatham) and to meet the Staff at the Mt. Elgin

> Residential School that was there . . . The opportunities at Muncey appealed to me immediately, and I was "hooked."

One chapter of his life was about to end, a new one would now begin. He could not have foreseen the consequences.

Interlude

VII A Bit of First Nations' History

It will be evident that the scope of Elgie's study of the problems in aboriginal education was, in the early stages, confined to a thorough knowledge of the reserves in southwestern Ontario. This was an area where the early pressures on native life were largely concentrated.

These pressures might have been lighter had there not been a large migration of Chippewas (the early "white" pronunciation of Ojibwa) into that fertile area. Huronia had been left almost empty by the Iroquois invasion so vividly portrayed by E. J. Pratt in *Brebeuf and His Brethren*. Then the Mohawks and Senecas dispersed the Neutrals, who had occupied the whole area from Lake Huron to about the present location of Oakville. Into this "vacuum" poured the Chippewas, originally from the Lake Superior area, along with some Delawares, Munsees, and Oneidas, all from New York State.

So the area was already occupied when the United Empire Loyalists migrated there seeking land after their expulsion from the United States. The Six Nations under Chief Joseph Brant had been allocated land along the Grand River. This area, the location of the first church (1785) in Upper Canada (Ontario), has been reduced by government sales. The money was to be kept in a trust fund for the reserve. A case is now (2001) before the courts to restore what seems to be lacking. Within about fifty years of the coming of the United Empire Loyalists the rest were confined to six reserves between the Grand River and Lakes Huron and St. Clair.

With the loss of their wide hunting grounds and original means of support, the problems that still face them emerged, underemployment and social conditions exacerbated by the white man's stock-in-trade, alcohol.

It seemed to many concerned church missionaries, and to some aboriginal leaders like Chief Peter Jones, that education was the answer. The Indians of Southern Ontario now lived in the white man's world, and they had to learn to adapt to that world. And the place to start was with the young. There were no schools—even for white settlers as yet.

There had been schools in Quebec long before this, but this early approach apparently was unknown in Ontario (Upper Canada).

A brief official account of early attempts to address the problem seems appropriate here. So I quote from the annual reports for 1936 and 1944 of the Department of Mines and Resources(!), Indian Affairs branch, which is also more extensively quoted in Bulletin 13 of the Ontario Department of Educational Research (pp. 15, 16):

> . . . All the early efforts with Indian children were wholly missionary in character. For nearly 200 years the work was carried on without financial aid from the Government. There is a record of Recollet Fathers' schools for Indian children in New France as early as 1616. . . . Prior to Confederation, day schools were successfully conducted at Lorette, St. Regis, and Pierreville in Lower Canada. At Caughnawaga educational work was made nearly impossible by local difficulties. However, there were interesting experiments at Chateauguay and Christieville, where Indian boys from Caughnawaga were taken into residence and given training in the classroom and on the farm . . . In Upper Canada, the Society for the Propagation of the Gospel organized the earliest Indian school (and the earliest school of any kind in Ontario, 1784) on the Tyendinaga Reserve on the Bay of Quinte. The New England Company, an evangelical organization, the Wesleyan Methodist Missionary Society, and the Jesuits interested themselves in Indian educational work in the early 19th century. Special institutions were established at this time: the Mohawk Institute by the New England Company, the Alderville and Mt. Elgin Boarding Schools by the Wesleyan Methodists, and the Wikwimikong Boarding School by the Jesuits. . . . Prior to Confederation there was practically no organization of Indian Schools in other parts of Canada.

Indian residential schools have come under severe attack in recent decades. So let us focus our historical survey on them, and in particular on one of the earliest, the Mt. Elgin Indian Residential School at Muncey, Ontario. It must be remembered that there were few day schools anywhere when it was founded in 1849; even by Confederation in 1867 there were only forty-nine in all of Canada. We shall consider their quality later.

Earlier we mentioned the concern of church leaders and some Indians for the future of aborigines in Southern Ontario who had been uprooted from their ancestral lands and way of life, and their belief that the solution lay in the education of the young. In seeking the best way to implement this, they looked, not to Quebec, but to a school begun in the United States in 1804 by a Presbyterian missionary among the Cherokees. To quote the historian John Webster Grant, the pattern he established was "a schedule that allotted equal time to study and work in the fields, shops, or kitchen of the institution. Several young Indians from Methodist missions attended such a school at Jacksonville, Illinois, and brought back enthusiastic reports. The system seemed to offer both a practical education and financial self-sufficiency" (*The Moon of Wintertime*, University of Toronto Press, p. 86).

He goes on to say that the Methodist leader, William Case, at Alderville (on the Rice Lake Reserve), adopted this plan in 1844. This received the enthusiastic advocacy of the governor-general, Lord Elgin, and led to the establishment in 1849 of a more ambitious school at Muncey, named, appropriately, The Mt. Elgin Institute. It had an interesting origin; at least in its beginning aborigines were involved.

The plan was conceived by the Rev. Peter Jones, an Ojibwa chief and minister of the Wesleyan Methodist Church, who was commissioned by the church in 1844 to visit England in search of the funds for a building. The Indians contributed to the project as well, especially in the gift of 200 acres of land for the school at Muncey. Portions of a letter by Mr. Jones reveal his purpose for the school:

> Our contemplated plans are to build two schools, one for 100 boys and one for 100 girls: the boys to be taught, in connection with a common English education, the art

> of farming and useful trades and the girls instructed in reading, writing, domestic economy, sewing, knitting and spinning so as to qualify them to be good wives and mothers. It is also our intention to select from these schools the most promising boys and girls, with a view to giving them superior advantages so as to qualify them for missionaries and school teachers among their brethren.

So the Mt. Elgin Institute came into being. It was the only residential school listed by the government of Canada in 1867, though there were a few others, notably the one in Brantford and the Roman Catholic boarding school at Wikwimikong, neither of which accepted government support and supervision. It operated for nearly a century.

In view of the spate of criticisms that such schools have received (there were seventy-five of them in all Canada by 1944), something should be said about their contribution to the well-being of Indians and of Canada. Here is a comment by Dr. Grant in his *The Moon of Wintertime* (University of Toronto Press, Toronto, 1984, p. 183):

> Despite its well-recognized weaknesses, Indian education should not be judged solely on the basis of its occasional horror stories. . . . Neat Western-styled homes and well-managed farms began to appear on some of the older reserves; more than half the members of the Queen Charlotte Council were Coquelestsa graduates. . . . Despite its shortcomings, the residential school evidently met a need.

Besides these general observations, let us note the specific advantages that an institute like Mt. Elgin (and by extension, other similar schools) offered Indian children:

> *Educationally*: grades were divided among three classrooms, with more specialized instruction. (Most day schools had only one.) Practical training was provided,

for the boys in shopwork, dairying, gardening and poultry, animal and field husbandry, and shoe repairing; for the girls in dietetics, serving of meals, housework, sewing, laundry, and music. Until curtailed by the war, instruction was given in special crafts, such as weaving and copper work. Attendance was more regular than it would have been on the reserve.

Physically: the pupils received a splendid foundation for later life, the product of regular hours, wholesome meals, and prompt care by a resident nurse and doctor.

Morally: the pupils were in the care of devoted workers, and the school was operated as a Christian institution. (Incidentally no charge of sexual abuse was ever levelled at Mt. Elgin.) Any criticism to the contrary, Mt. Elgin Residential School has made a significant contribution to the life of the Indian people.

(Bulletin #13, Ontario Department of Education, p. 64)

The man who wrote these commendations was Elgie Joblin. Nevertheless, in 1947, armed with a telling list of the disadvantages of residential education and a comprehensive plan for greatly improved day schools, he persuaded the Indian Affairs department and the United Church of Canada to discontinue Mt. Elgin and initiate a pilot program in Indian education for the six reserves of Western Ontario. So the work of Canada's premier Indian residential school ended after ninety-eight years, decades before mounting criticism focused attention on a system that had long been accepted.

Now we are ready to speak of Elgie's work at the Caradoc Reservation at Muncey, one of six reserves in southwestern Ontario west of the Six Nation (Iroquois) Reserve at Brantford.

Second Movement

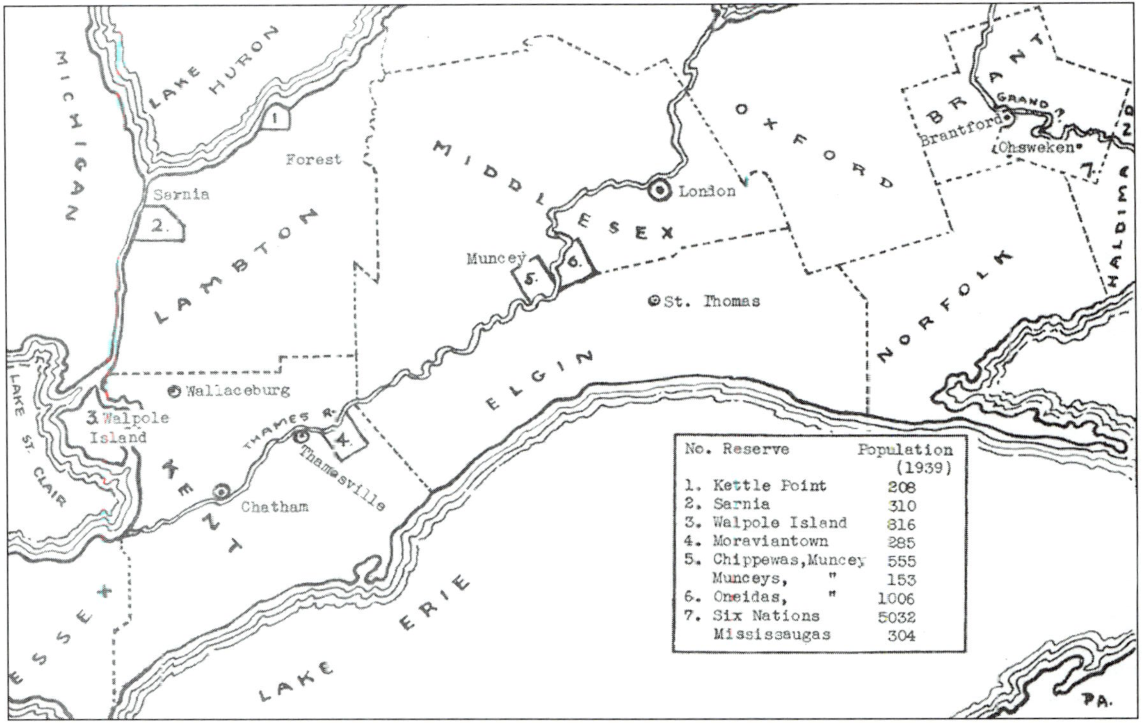

1. Location of Indian Reserves of Western Ontario

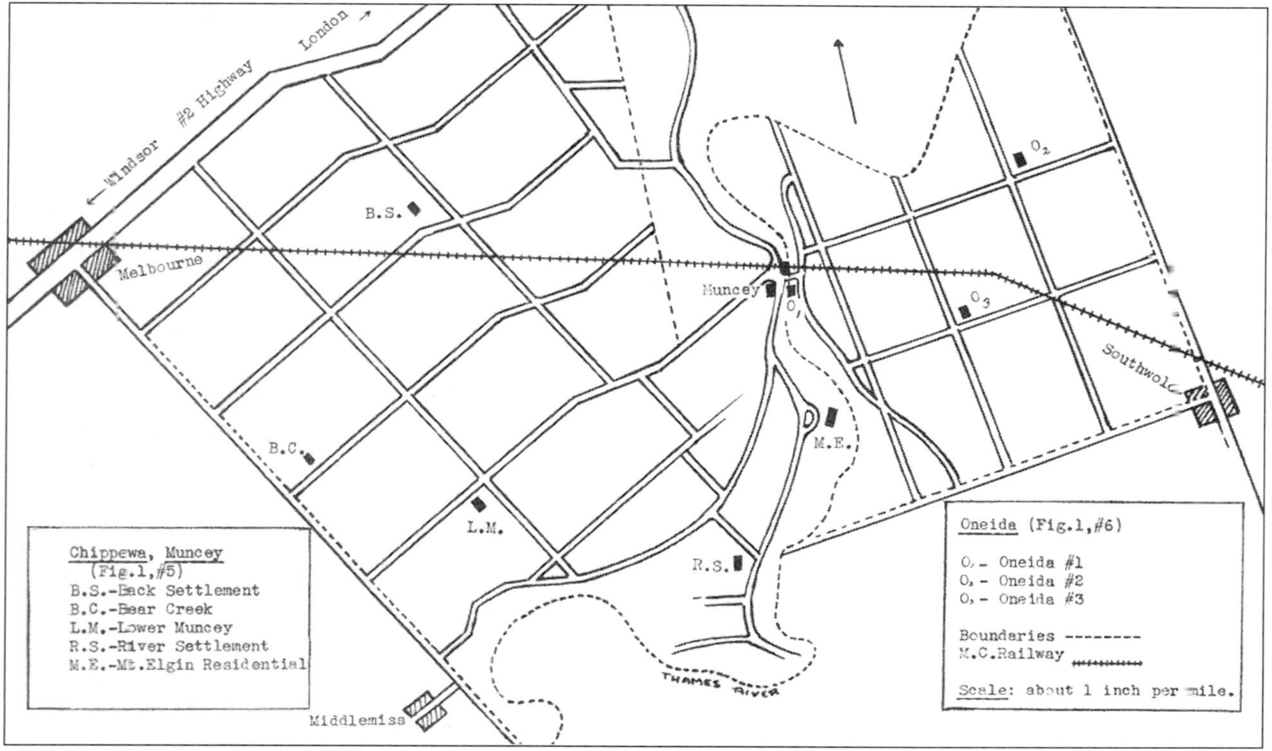

2. Location of Schools on the Reserves at Muncey

Theme One: Serving First Nations as Minister

VIII Eight Busy Years

Eight years was four times as long as most missionaries had stayed. But they were happy and busy years for Elgie. Whether such isolation was also happy for Helen she never said. At least they were together at last. So, did they rush into the blessed state of matrimony immediately after his ordination?

No, Elgie still had a few weeks at Wesley-Curve Lake. He was busy with weddings and baptisms that had awaited his ordination. Then there must have been the matter of money. At $7.00 a week, how much could he save to start supporting a wife? Finally, the old manse needed a lot of repairs before bringing a bride into it. I marveled later at the remodeling of the kitchen, which he probably enjoyed doing.

The day finally came: October 21st, 1936. A host of folk would have liked to attend. Not only the families, but old friends from Stirling, Mt. Pleasant Church, Cordova, and Wesley-Curve Lake. How many were invited? None. Only their parents knew—and even they were not asked. I suppose this reflected their lifestyle, before and after.

So the attendance was the minimum required plus one. There had to be a minister; as assistant at Deer Park United I could supply the chapel. There had to be two witnesses. Our sister Gladys was the bridesmaid; a college friend, Charles Kitney, was best man. The plus one? No occasion in Elgie's life would be complete without music, and Harold Kitney supplied that on the chapel organ. The honeymoon was a week at the cottage.

It was soon evident that the happy couple had their work cut out for them. The manse (or "mission house" to the Indians) was isolated, poorly furnished, and without electricity or telephone. This was Helen's domain, and she would make the most of it. There was a garden long neglected, which Elgie would coax into full productivity, and a barn, well populated with rats—no great problem after the infestation of Bayside. There was also a chicken house to which Elgie immediately introduced hens bought from the residential school. They produced much of the needed protein—not only the eggs, but the meat preserved in large sealers. (The local store sold only the "long clear" [fat pork] and "Muncey ham" [bologna] which the Indians could afford in those depression days.) Eventually he bought a cow, and a series of little pigs to use the extra milk. Since even by 1940 his salary was only $1,200.00 a year, they needed to be as self-sustaining as possible.

So much for the domestic arrangements; now for the work Elgie was called to do. There were four churches, serving two different "nations," and a smaller group, the Munceys. On one side of the Thames River were two Chippewa churches, Colborne and Little Bear Creek. These folk were of the same basic stock of Ojibwas as the Mississaugas of Curve Lake. On the other side were two Oneida churches, representing an Iroquois tribe who had emigrated from New York State around 1840. Like Kipling's East and West, the two groups had little to do with each other. Elgie began to break down the barriers by organizing a baseball league among the several schools. In the playoffs there was a lot of mingling of parents. Then he suggested a united picnic for all four churches that was a real success. Incidentally, he had to provide transportation for whole baseball teams. He built a trailer with benches, took the lid off the old Plymouth's large trunk, and supplied it with cushions. What would safety officials say now about this?

These folk whose origins were so far away had something basic in common: they had all been converted to Methodist Christianity in the mid-nineteenth century. And they still maintained many old Methodist customs, such as the exhorters at prayer meetings. For these—and for parts of the Sunday services—they still used their own languages, which Elgie encouraged. Often the only English used (though they all understood it) was Elgie's meditation and prayer. Their eloquence and obvious sincerity impressed him. They would have been inhibited if expected to use English.

Another old Methodist custom still flourished here and on other reserves: the camp meeting. Elgie was surprised when the smallest group of all, at Bear Creek, sponsored one. People came from far and near, bringing their own local preachers and exhorters. The meetings went on, morning, afternoon, and evening, for a week. Perhaps riding that momentum they decided to move an old hall—perhaps once a lodge—to the back of their little church. Now they could have their own socials, since their homes were too small for many visitors at a time and guests had to sit on the floor.

These "socials" provided the entertainment for each of the four areas. There was little planning. Singers, fiddlers, or storytellers would provide impromptu numbers. Elgie with his piano accordion could lead a singsong. The climax of the evening was the food, contributed by all who came. With four churches, Helen was kept busy with her share of the food. One woman told her she always got one of her sandwiches—they were made with red salmon. They couldn't afford that for themselves—nor could the Joblins.

At the Colborne Church there were few young people in attendance, so Elgie started a games night that proved popular. Quite a few began coming to church, and some joined the choir. In all the activities, religious and social, his aim was to have the Indians develop initiative and do things for themselves. His conviction was that white men had always done things *for* the Indians, whereas they should have done things *with* them.

So we come to the biggest joint venture of all: joining the two Oneida congregations together and building one new church that would have ample space for social gatherings, clinics, and all the things that the old single-room churches could not accommodate. What discussions must have gone on in each congregation separately, and then with both together! Gradually they warmed to the idea, though they knew what it would involve. Elgie worked with an architect, and the plan was approved by the presbytery. They asked the Board of Home Missions for a grant of $10,000.00—and were given $7,000.00. I could say here that its head, Dr. R. B. Cochrane, had a reputation among the ministerial students for closefistedness. We should have remembered that the Great Depression had taken its toll on general church finances.

They couldn't build the kind of church that was needed for $7,000.00. What to do? First, organize both congregations into volunteer brigades. Second, persuade Uncle Fred Elgie, who now had a contracting business in Belleville, to postpone all projects, pile his equipment into his truck, and come to supervise the work on day-wage pay. Uncle Fred was the soul of generosity; his know-how and cheerfulness won over the Indians, and the work began.

Men who belonged to the two churches tore them down carefully and brought the material to the site, where women sorted and piled it, cleaned the bricks, pulled the nails and straightened them. The church was to have two layers of solid brick, and only the outside layer had new bricks. Meanwhile, other men were excavating the basement and putting in the foundation. When the building was up, a young Indian, trained as an electrician though unemployed, did all the wiring and accepted no remuneration. This was an act of faith; there was no power on that side of the river. The Hydro was persuaded to bring it across and hook it up for $200.00.

Of course there were all sorts of logistics to work out, ordering and so on. This was Elgie's job. But he was happier when he could work along with his men. What about Sunday services for the two congregations? The pews from the old churches were set up on the manse lawn, and simply turned over afterward to shed the rain. A shelter was set up near the job, and the women prepared meals so no time would be lost going home. What a hive of activity it must have been, and what spirit of camaraderie was developed!

Even with all Elgie's fund-raising efforts (I know he tapped the family!) such as choir concerts in London churches, the money ran out and he had to borrow $1,000.00 to finish the job. But what a splendid job it was: a beautiful sanctuary, and a full basement with kitchen for mid-week meetings, socials, even clinics for such things as vaccination. At the dedication on December 14th, 1941, Dr. George Dorey preached at two services. Elgie's parents were there, and it must have been a proud moment for them as for everyone else. Elgie quoted from Nehemiah's account of building the walls of Jerusalem: "So we built the wall, for the people had a mind to work." A visiting First Nations entertainer who had traveled widely in the United States and Canada said that it was the finest aboriginal church she had ever seen.

IX *Wampum*

From the first, Elgie believed that the sense of isolation of men and women in situations like his was bad for morale. Moreover, each one had experience and knowledge to share that would be helpful. He took three steps to address these needs. In his holidays he visited each mission in southwestern Ontario. An Indian Missionaries' Association was formed. The most important thing—and one that was to demand much thought and effort—was the establishment of a quarterly magazine to contain news from each reserve, helpful ideas from the missionaries, articles of interest, and so on. He was appointed editor. "It's a great idea. You do it."

He chose to call it *Wampum*, naming it for the medium of exchange (belts of intricately patterned tiny shells) used for intertribal communication before the advent of the white man. It was a one-man production, except for the material sent in. Two hundred copies were needed when the demand increased. He wrote an editorial, typed the material, cut the stencils, wrapped and mailed each copy. If content were short, he included excerpts from our father's interesting diary from the early years of the century when he was missionary-teacher at Norway House and Cross Lake, Manitoba. Each subscription cost 25 cents a year. I quote from his journal:

> The quarterly issue ran to between 10 to 15 pages. The ministers serving Indian charges in Western Ontario received theirs in quantities for distribution, all others were individually wrapped and mailed. There were subscribers in most provinces and several States as well as one in New Zealand.

He kept this up for ten years, including two years after he resigned and took up special education in Toronto. His dedication to the magazine is illustrated by this excerpt from his journal:

> All quarterly issues were met during the two years of my stay in Toronto when I had a very demanding workload. But the one that proved to be the most strenuous was the one dated January 1st, 1945 prepared during the Christmas season. There was a very heavy snowstorm that year that tied up all traffic, just when I was trying to get *Wampum* done. The stencils had been run off and were ready for me at 299 Queen Street West (United Church H.Q. then) but there was no way to get them home except by carrying them in two suitcases, on foot, from Queen Street, up Spadina to Bloor, across to Madison Avenue, and 3 blocks north, with snow often up to my knees. Those cases held up to 2400 sheets of paper 8 1/2 x 11, and I think even the reading material must have been heavy. But the paper went out on time... There is a complete set in the United Church Archives. They contain, for their time, a most remarkable collection of contributions from a wide range of interested people.

Before we get to *that* strenuous period, and after the even more strenuous building of the new Oneida United Church, perhaps a brief description of quiet domestic life is in order. When Dad suffered a serious heart attack in 1942 and had to resign from the Scugog charge with its small Indian reserve, he and Mother first stayed with brother Fred and his bride Audrey in the manse at Bowmanville, Ontario. It could have been our turn next, but we were already looking after Pat's mother and had two children, so there was no room with us. Instead they had a happy visit with Elgie and Helen, with Dad regaining his strength as he walked the country roads. Mother was delighted with the prospect of a visit, and not least for a peculiar reason. All her life as a rural minister's wife she had wanted a Jersey cow. At last there was one in the family. She insisted on milking it. It resisted. That Jersey would not "give" to the stranger no matter how hard she tried. Life is full of disappointments.

Interlude: "Sell All You Have."

X A New Venture

Perhaps this heading should include . . . of Faith. This Abraham believed his next step was a response to a Call, and there was no certainty of arriving at a hoped-for destination. It was not a sudden decision: much thought and research preceeded it.

Elgie's conviction, derived from his four years experience at Curve Lake Reserve, was that little could be accomplished by short-term ministries. His journal had reported that his arrival at Muncey had caused scarcely a ripple. There had been a succession of "missionaries," all sent without consultation with the Indians. He was an exception. He stayed on the job eight years. The new church was only a visible sign of his success; the later years showed an increasing number of new members received on Profession of Faith, most of them adults. Even now, when he resigned as their minister, he hoped that he would return to them in a new "incarnation." We need to follow the steps that led to this hope.

From the first he was interested in the pupils of the eight schools on the Caradoc Reserve (the name of the township in which Muncey is located). He got to know them through the sports programs he initiated. So he readily became interested in the work of the schools and their teachers. The picture they presented disturbed him. The teachers worked without adequate equipment and lacked sufficient training for this specialized work. If their morale was low, there were reasons. The results of their work were discouraging, and we shall see why presently. They were isolated and mostly lived in inadequate housing. Salaries were low with no incremental raises to induce them to stay. Elgie's reports to the Board of Home Missions pointed all this out, though little could be done unless the Department of Indian Affairs cooperated.

The chance for *him* to do something about it came in 1945, during his seventh year on the reserve. At that time "Indian Affairs" was merely a branch of the Federal Department of Mines and Resources. Spurred by a report from engineers that the condition of the "Mt. Elgin Industrial Institute" was unsatisfactory and by their opinion that the cost per pupil was excessive in view of the results, they set up a commission of three to investigate all the reserves that sent pupils to Mt. Elgin. In particular, they were to decide what would be done on the Caradoc Reserve should the institute be abolished. One member was W. S. Arneil, inspector of Indian Agencies for Ontario. The second was Gordon Young, the inspector of schools. The third was Elgie, who represented the interests of the United Church, which worked in partnership with the department on all the reserves to be visited. He was nominated because of his obvious interest in Indian education, and since he was already known and trusted on the reserves because of his voluntary visits and interest in them. No doubt his knowledge of the work of the institute and his excellent relations with its staff were added reasons.

Gordon Young and Elgie were charged with producing this commission's report, and they spent many hours preparing it. Very few students, except at Mt. Elgin, graduated from Grade VIII. The suggestion that Indians in general were not fitted for higher academic studies was refuted by the excellent record of schools at the Six Nations Reserve near Brantford. The fault lay elsewhere, in poor buildings, over-burdened and under-prepared teachers, lack of parental interest, frequent absences because parents moved in search of employment, lack of special curriculums—and so the list goes on.

The buildings were the easiest to assess. None had indoor privies or electricity, but neither did most rural schools in Ontario then. All but one had inadequate window lighting. One, at Kettle Point, had two rooms, but it was overcrowded by the addition of pupils from Stoney Point. It sent sixteen to Mt. Elgin. The only other two-room school was at Walpole Island, which had another one-room frame school. Only five from here went to Mt. Elgin. At St. Clair the senior students were bussed into Sarnia, giving the teacher needed relief. The Moraviantown school was well built but had forty-three students representing many grades.

The worst situation was on the Chippewa and Muncey side of the Thames on the Caradoc Reserve. The Lower Muncey School had been closed for lack of enough pupils. Bear Creek had been closed at different times for lack of a teacher. The Back Settlement School had burned down some time ago, and the pupils met in the basement of the Anglican Church. On the Oneida Reserve on the east side, the three schools were somewhat better, with an enrollment of 101.

The Mt. Elgin Residential School requires further discussion, though we dealt with its positive side as noted in Elgie's earlier assessment. Through its nearly one hundred years it had made a great contribution to the lives of Indians who had to make the transition from a hunter-gatherer culture to the new rural-agricultural and mechanical lifestyle. But it had never fulfilled its founder's hopes. (See *Sacred Feathers: The Biography of Chief Peter Jones*, by Donald B. Smith, University of Toronto Press, Toronto, 1988.) He had hoped that it would provide educated personnel to operate it, but it had always been and still was run entirely by whites. The original building (1849) was still in use, with classrooms on the ground floor and staff apartments above. By now it had been condemned as unsound. The later building could house 150, but it too needed renovation.

Elgie appreciated the work its staff was doing, and he was respected by all as its unofficial chaplain. But he could not be blind to its present weaknesses, and these were listed in the commission's report. Even though the lack of day schools in the earlier decades in Western Ontario seemed to justify a central school, he felt it was a mistake to uproot the children from their homes, teach them only in English, and send them back to the reserves strangers to their own culture. Nowadays there were too many in the lower grades, though at least there were three classrooms. Many of these should have been with their own families, inadequate though home conditions might have been. There were fewer older students due to lack of space, so there was too much work for them on the farm, though it taught them good agricultural methods and supplied much of the produce needed to support the school. (The government per capita grants were too small.)

Another difficulty was that Indian agencies had the habit of sending their problem children to the better-supervised residential school. These students resented the new discipline and made the development of school spirit difficult. There was little time for recreation or vocational guidance, no schooling past Grade VIII, and no follow-up or placement on leaving school. How could the report justify Mt. Elgin's continuation in view of the high costs and needed repairs? (The complete story of Mt. Elgin as recorded by Elgie is in the United Church archives.)

Yet the problems of the day schools were not limited to teaching all grades in inadequate buildings. In view of the later recommendations in his book *The Education of the Indians of Western Ontario*, it is worthwhile to quote some of his conclusions about these problems (p. 66 ff):

> A really good teacher *with adequate training* will create an effective situation for the guidance of learning in spite of inadequate equipment or curriculum . . . The crux of the problem is to be found here. The teachers have been doing what they were trained to do, but with a growing sense of failure and frustration. The training of teachers in Ontario is in need of revision. (I note here that much of this has since been done.) A one-year's course at Normal School is insufficient. The training is principally in devices and techniques plus the mastery of subject matter; the psychology of learning has not been given its true place.

He then goes on to say that more guidance ought to be given for the specific task of teaching Indian children, who were unused to regimentation and authoritarianism. Rows of immovable seats, enforced quiet, and memorization of material militate against a happy environment and stultify creativity. Another problem that he had discovered regarding the situation on his own reserve was the failure of teachers to identify with the parents of their pupils. In view of their workloads this was understandable. But the teachers needed parental cooperation in stressing the values of education and in overcoming absenteeism. The problem would not be so acute if the teachers themselves were Indian. But "any white person must break down a barrier of suspicion and distrust toward himself on the part of the Indian people before he can hope to accomplish anything on their behalf." He had practiced what he preached in his own ministry.

All of this was adumbrated in the report of the Commission to the Department of Indian Affairs. They were eager to initiate immediately one of its recommendations—the discontinuation of the Mt. Elgin Residential School. Elgie, backed by the Board of Home Missions, insisted that this should not be done until an adequate day-school system be put in its place. They consented, probably reluctantly. But who should design and implement a new plan for the Caradoc Reserve that could be a pilot for other reserves?

We have spoken earlier of Elgie's "Call" to the ministry. We speak of a person's "calling." No doubt everyone should have such a sense leading to their choice of work. Elgie had a second Call—to an educational ministry. It was to lead to a radical change in his life.

No doubt he had wished for years that there could be changes in the education of youth both at the residential school and in the day schools. But as a result of the commission's visits and consultations, it dawned on him that perhaps *he* should do something about it. If the pilot project were to be at Muncey, it would be helpful if the director knew the situation and had the confidence of the people. The same was true about the abolition of the residential school—it should be done with a minimum of friction; it had been part of the community for nearly 100 years. And there was another reason: for all that time the Methodist and the United Churches had served the reserve, and he did not think the time was ripe for complete secularization.

He was willing to prepare himself to direct the radical changes he envisioned. He talked it over with the institute's principal, the Rev. O. B. Strapp, his long-time friend and one who would be most affected by change. There had been enough hints from the Department of Indian Affairs that the end was in sight for the old school. The principal knew he was not prepared to take charge of a new system, and he encouraged Elgie to "go for it." The inspector, Gordon Young, also encouraged him, but warned that he would get nowhere with the department without a degree in education. The Board of Home Missions would be sorry to lose their faithful missionary but raised no objections, though they pointed out that there was no guarantee of an appointment at the end of the trail.

With this encouragement, and Helen's backing, he burned his bridges and ended twelve years as a minister to Indians.

Beside all the farewells there was a project that he saw to completion. During that final year he had offered to supervise the boys in all the day schools in a course in woodwork. The final exhibition of their work was a credit to all and showed what they could do with a little guidance.

Financing was a problem for him. When he had consulted with Dr. Lewis of the College of Education in Toronto, he had been offered an assistantship (half-time) at $75.00 a month. Then, acting as auctioneer, he and Helen sold off everything they could not take in the trailer: her precious piano; the family cow and pig; and the furniture and kitchen things they had bought, including a two-burner Coleman gas stove. They made enough to pay off $800.00 still owing on his college debt. Then off they went to a new (and spartan!) life with $400.00 and an old car that had to be stopped frequently to fill up the leaking radiator with water. Abraham brought more with him when setting out for his Promised Land.

XI A Busy Interlude

Priority number one—at least in Helen's mind—was a place to live. Solution: a little room and tiny kitchen originally intended for a maid, in the apartment of the widow of Principal Davidson of Emmanuel College. With a purchased studio couch that pulled out for night use (one side was very hard; I know because I bought it when they left), it became a bedroom, living room, and study. This was not luxury living. But it had three advantages: it was cheap; it was near the College of Education (Madison Avenue runs off Bloor Street near Spadina) and, best of all, Mrs. Davidson took Helen under her wing so that Elgie did not have to worry about her isolation. She had a very happy year, for once with few responsibilities.

He needed all the time he could get. His assistantship involved some supervision of the work of younger students, and he was enrolled in the M.A. course in the "Philosophy and Psychology of Elementary School" subjects. He was pleased also with his two minor courses. One was "Occupations and Vocational Guidance," material he hoped to have the chance to apply if given the chance. The other was "Anthropology" with Dr. T. F. McIlwraith at the museum. This would give him a better understanding of Canadian aborigines.

This should have been enough. But he kept in touch with the workers on the reserves of Western Ontario, and still edited the *Wampum* (and did everything else to get the finished product out). Moreover, he signed on as an occasional "casual" worker, unloading bags of flour from a boxcar for a bakery on Dupont Street. He said the exercise was good for him.

The highlight of the first term was attending the Eastern Regional Conference of the Fellowship of Indian Workers, held one weekend in October in Iroquois, N.Y. It was to be the first of many such conferences held in different parts of the U.S.A. He found it a stimulating experience. He also met many gifted Indian Christians like the Rev. David W. Owl. His own paper on Indian work in southwestern Ontario was well received, according to Dr. George Dorey who drove his car to the conference and took Elgie. They became good friends.

On Sundays, which most students used to work on overdue essays, he and Helen visited various city churches, an opportunity he had not had since his second year in arts. His favourite was Metropolitan United. He admired Dr. Peter Bryce not only for his preaching, but for his work in social programmes for the poor of downtown Toronto.

The new situation also made it possible to visit more frequently with Helen's mother and with the senior Joblins. He had helped discover a very suitable house for his parents in Port Perry with a bedroom and an essential luxury (if that is not a contradiction in terms), a toilet, on the ground floor. Sister Gladys, always ready to give up personal advantage for the family, resigned from her teaching job in Bowmanville and found one in Port Perry so she could look after Mother and Dad. Younger sister Dorothy, who was teaching in Pickering, gave up *her* weekends to lend a hand, taking on the washing and ironing as her contribution. I confess that brother Fred and I came off best in this filial arrangement. Occasional help in the large garden was apparently the best we could do. The new home became a sort of centre for all of us. Mother and Dad had their first home ever. Mother could rejoice in her first bathroom, plus electric lights and telephone. I donated a radio and Mother reveled in its classical music, especially Toscanini and his symphony. Dad's former parishioners from Scugog Island could visit him, and he was soon able to start a Bible class in the nearby church. In spite of health problems they had many happy years in this ideal setting, which they were convinced was the gift of Providence. I was reminded of a verse from Psalm 16 that Dad had often used in our family prayers: "The lines have fallen to me in pleasant places."

After this excursus into family affairs, let us return to Elgie's new academic efforts. At the end of the college year, he visited all the reserve schools in southwestern Ontario to administer a series of tests he had devised with the help of his adviser. He believed that the children enjoyed these breaks from the routine of learning, and was quite sure the teachers did. He knew each one of them personally from previous visits and from long correspondence in the preparation of *Wampum*. At each stop he and Helen were entertained by these old friends, exchanging news and ideas. The only expense on the trip was for gasoline. The water for the leaky radiator was free.

Most of the vacation was spent analyzing the results of this research and preparing and tabulating all sorts of other information pertaining to

Indian education. In his final submission that appeared as Bulletin #13 of the Department of Educational Research, I counted forty (yes, forty!) charts, tables, graphs, and maps, along with a careful explanation of each. Those who dealt with such things in the department must have been pleased.

Now he was faced with the second year of his program, with some courses but with the major effort the writing of the M.A. thesis. His $75.00 assistantship was renewed, but the $400.00 from the sale of assets was gone. What now? He sold the beloved cottage on Buckhorn Lake to the granddaughter of the Harrises with whom he had boarded and from whom he had bought the lot. The selling price was $800.00, the cost of the materials that had gone into it. There is not a word of regret in his journal. The rest of the family lamented for him.

There was another problem. Mrs. Davidson had moved to smaller accommodations. Where would they go? We offered to share our house in Weston, but travel in and out would be time-consuming. Again Providence provided. A college friend, the Rev. Arthur Kewley, was called to St. Clair Avenue United Church. He and Fay had two children and another was expected. But their house on Bracondale Road was large and had two empty rooms on the third floor. They were soon full. So began what his journal called the happiest year of their lives together. They had been denied children of their own. Katherine, Allen, and baby Anne became their family too. And not for that year only, but for the rest of their lives. While living there, Helen insisted on doing the washing and ironing, and was a ready "sitter" when Fay was at church meetings. As usual, Elgie was away all day and at his typewriter most evenings. But there was no question of Helen languishing in practical isolation on the third floor. She was part of the family.

During his research in these two years he had amassed an exhaustive bibliography of all aspects of Indian education and culture. The department found this of such value that it was issued as Educational Research Series #15. Though updated since then, it remains a standard resource.

In the second year there was less course work, so he decided to work on his Bachelor of Divinity degree in Emmanuel College, provided he could tie it in with his concerns. This was possible through the help of his supervisor, Prof. Fred Langford, who taught Christian education. There were two minor courses and a major. The one he found most rewarding was again with Professor T. F. McIlwraith of the Department of Anthropology. The resulting thesis, "Early or Primitive Religion Among the Indians and Inuit of Canada," is on file in the Library of Emmanuel College.

At the College of Education, a course he found particularly helpful was a new one being developed by a Mr. Parmenter for secondary schools on occupations and vocational guidance. When Elgie was appointed to his new work at Muncey (a point at which this narrative will also shortly arrive), he set up an intermediate school for Grades VII to X. Any pupils who had previously made it to that point, and there were few, had had to go elsewhere. He taught this vocation course himself for the following eleven years, and had the satisfaction of inspiring many who went on to higher achievements.

As the proverb puts it, all good things come to an end. For the convocation where he was awarded his M.A. he bought a hood—and never wore it again. For the Emmanuel Convocation, the B.D. hood was borrowed.

These degrees were but means to an end. The Department of Indian Affairs, impressed by his thesis, accepted the recommendation of the Board of Home Missions. His new life was about to begin.

The "job description" that came with his appointment on July 1st, 1946, was a daunting one. In part it was to establish a pilot project that might be followed elsewhere. He was determined that it should succeed. He was to be the principal and part-time teacher, of a new senior school at Muncey. He was also to be the superintendent of schools for all the other schools on the reserve. A tall order indeed!

Basically, the department in Ottawa accepted the proposals in his M.A. thesis, which was printed as Bulletin #13 of the Department of Educational Research and widely distributed. Each one of the eight recommendations was carefully argued in the thesis. We will quote them verbatim (pp. 48-50):

Summary of Recommendations

> To ensure equality of opportunity to the Indians of Western Ontario and the type of education they require

for this critical period of transition, the following recommendations have been made:

That a *single administrative unit* for the purposes of education be made of the five Reserves included in the survey (Kettle Point, Sarnia, Walpole Island, Moraviantown, and Muncey), and that a *Superintendent of Schools* be appointed for this area.

That day schools be developed as *community service centres*; that those of the first four reserves be *two-room schools*. That the Mt. Elgin Indian Residential School as such be discontinued, and a *Senior School* or Junior High School be built on the property at Muncey.

That the *teachers* for these schools be carefully selected from among the best in the province on the basis of their personal qualifications, training, and previous successful experience. To make this possible, other provisions must be made: (a) Inducements. Salaries must at least equal those of the town schools of Ontario and provide an increase for satisfactory service; there must be membership in a Pension Plan, either in the Civil Service or Teachers' and Inspectors' Superannuation Fund of Ontario; living and teaching conditions must be made attractive; (b) In-service training must be made obligatory, including regular Summer School courses in Kindergarten-Primary, Auxiliary classes, educational psychology and related subjects; a Summer School for teachers of Indian Schools should be held the first week in September, as well as monthly meetings of teachers for study and fellowship. Supervision should be more thorough, helpful, and encouraging.

That the methods of the *Activity Programme* be thoroughly studied and applied, and that materials and equipment be adjusted to facilitate this type of classroom procedure. That assistance be given those teachers who will use to advantage the Audio-Visual Aids now available.

That the *Curriculum* of the Province be accepted, with adaptations made by the teacher on the basis of pupil needs. Grades I to VI should be of a general and basic character, with emphasis on the mastery of spoken English and Reading. Grades VII to IX should be provided in the two-room schools, with opportunity for High School Entrance, but emphasis on the optional subjects for those who will go no further. At Muncey, the day schools should include only Grades I to VI, pupils to be admitted to the Senior School at twelve years of age or after completion of Grade VI.

The Senior School should specialize in Grades VII to X, both academic and vocational, but include classes for Grades I to VI. Classification of senior pupils should be by their year in the school rather than by grade. There should be development of the following courses, Home Economics, Commercial, Agriculture, Building Trades, Motor Mechanics, and other practical work as the demand arises.

Pupils should have the opportunity of part-time work and educational training from 16 to 18 years of age. The possibilities of apprenticeship in the building trades should be investigated. Social and recreational activities should be encouraged, and the leadership available when needed.

That a programme of *Educational and Vocational Guidance and Placement* be developed and directed by the Superintendent of Schools with the co-operation of the teachers. That this programme include responsibility for pre-school children and graduates, as well as those of school age.

That a serious consideration be given to making the advantages of the Senior School Available to pupils of reserves other than Muncey, by the provision of residential accommodation of a kind suitable to "teen-age" young people (i.e. until such schools are available in those reserves).

That the Senior School be free of denominational bias; the United Church of Canada, while retaining its voice in the broader policies of the school, may surrender some of its prerogatives in the interests of the total good of the Indian people.

(It is surprising that he did not include the teaching of the pupils' native traditions and culture. He did this in his own work.)

Theme Two: Serving First Nations as Superintendent of Schools

XII Getting Started

The newly appointed superintendent/principal/teacher and his wife arrived back in Muncey on June 30th, 1946. Not at the old manse, however. The original Mt. Elgin building, now nearly a century old, was still there, with two apartments on the second floor. Mr. and Mrs. Gordon Long, from the staff of the now-defunct residential school, occupied one. He was to stay long enough to help Elgie dispose of its assets. The Joblins took over the other, and there they stayed for four years. There is no record of what Helen thought of this. We had always thought that she had a rather nervous disposition. But here she was, upstairs in a building that had long been condemned as unsafe, and whose walls were bolstered by huge 12 x 12 supports. Readers may already have been impressed by her fulfillment of the assertion in the Book of Ruth: "Where thou lodgest I will lodge."

The two men packed up and sent off everything that could be used by the residential schools still in operation in the West, and then auctioned off everything else. Elgie bought things that were needed in their apartment, including, to her joy, a piano for Helen to replace her own, which they had sold two years before.

Then the real work began. He visited all the school districts of the Caradoc Reserve, and listed forty-three names of pupils ready for a senior school. It was just as well that he had this information. On August 13th "top-level" officials from Ottawa came to discuss the situation. They met first with Mr. Downs, the Indian agent. He persuaded them that a senior school could not possibly begin for another year: construction of the new building had not even started; no teachers had been hired; no buses were ready; roads had not been regraded . . . Then they came to see Elgie with this decision. He was appalled. It meant the loss of a year for most if not all of the forty-three pupils, since they did not intend to go to the local one-room schools. Elgie argued down Mr. Downs. There were three classrooms still ready in the old building; one former teacher was willing to take charge, a Mr. Johnston from Thorold Residential School; Elgie would teach until a second could be hired; transportation could surely be arranged by schooltime . . . He won.

There was a delay in getting the school year under way. During part of this time he called the teachers together for a "consultation" in which he discussed his ideals and hopes. This was a first for them, and after initial misgivings about the length of time slated, they became enthusiastic. Apparently the parents were pleased too; this was tobacco harvest time; they took their children with them and the older ones helped. Finally, Elgie secured the use of an idled ambulance; the Anglican priest brought in the pupils from the Back Settlement. The pilot project began. Mr. Downs was not amused but had a bus available the next week.

Perhaps Elgie felt the need to justify opposing the Indian agent; at any rate he included in his journal the story of two of the students who profited from that first year, when he "jumped the gun." One was an Oneida girl who had dropped out of Grade X in the continuation school at Delaware because she could not make it in mathematics. She had dreamed of becoming a nurse. Elgie found out from her teachers that there was little hope she could pass in Grade IX, let alone XI and XII. Are some people constitutionally ill adapted to math, or is it a failure in the teaching of lower grades? Elgie went to the hospital in St. Thomas. They worked out a plan to substitute other subjects for mathematics as entrance requirements. She came to the Muncey School; Elgie tutored her. She did well, graduated from the nursing school at the St. Thomas Hospital, and served there for years.

Another student from that first year was a local Oneida boy who had also dropped out of Delaware. He enrolled at Muncey, got his Grade X, and enlisted in the Navy. When he retired he took the United Church course for local preachers in Middlesex presbytery, and was in considerable demand there. Of course there is no guarantee that students with problems will become success stories. Teachers may wait years before their efforts are justified. Their work requires patience and faith.

A second teacher was found on November 19th of that first year, freeing the principal for another experiment, which he called an "opportunity class." Teachers in the one-room schools (now up to Grade VI) had little time for the slow learners—or should we call them the educationally challenged? Those aged twelve or over were bused to Muncey and put into this special class in the third room of the old building. No longer with younger children, and with the encouragement of a teacher who had studied child psychology, they made better progress. Elgie continued this class for a number of years. That first year showed him the complexity of the task, so instead of taking holidays in July and August, he took the provincial summer course in auxiliary education at Jarvis Collegiate in Toronto. He found it a very useful experience, especially in the use of crafts and music to stimulate learning.

This desire to equip himself fully for his work had led him to postpone for a year the two full summer schools he had to take in order to secure his First Class certificate with its much better pay schedule. Did Helen question his priorities? *Some* wives would, but there is no mention of it. In regard to further qualifications, the records show that he was admitted to the "Doctor of Education" course in May of 1952, and that he spent that summer in attendance at the College of Education. There is no mention of further follow-up.

XIII In Full Swing

We have written that one of Elgie's accomplishments while minister at Muncey was the editing of *Wampum*, thus helping overcome the sense of isolation that the missionaries scattered through southwest Ontario must have felt. Now there was a similar venture in communications for the teachers and parents on the Caradoc Reserve. The archive collection of this weekly *School News* provides a full record of all that went on in the years that followed. We can only mention a few high points.

New teachers were introduced in this way. He was particularly pleased to get back Mrs. Marjorie Docker who had left Bear Creek for Mt. Brydges. She stayed throughout his time there and was an enthusiastic supporter. For instance: after a new venture, taking the students to the interschool Track and Field Day at Mt. Brydges, the students did well at sports (especially at ball, which he had been coaching for years) but were a failure at the social evening that followed. The same unwillingness to participate was evident when they were invited to a Hallowe'en party at Lambeth United Church. So Elgie bought some records, and Mrs. Docker taught them several square dance routines. Then, when they were invited to a youth social evening at our brother Fred's Wesley Church in London, they demonstrated these and then took part with the others. This was a giant step out of their isolation.

In May of 1947 the department in Ottawa had approved the new venture, including bringing all pupils twelve or over to the central school. So its plans were finalized, providing four classrooms and a full basement with washrooms and adequate space for household science and manual training. Construction began. In that same May, Elgie was given a task that required much preparation. He was asked to speak at the annual meeting of the Women's Missionary Society in a Toronto United church. It is obvious why he was chosen. The two residential schools that they sponsored in Saskatchewan were to be closed by the government. The women were anxious and troubled. Elgie had put a positive "spin" on the closing of the Mt. Elgin Institute, and he did so on this occasion. There is no mention of it in his journal, but the text of his address is extant. It reflects his own experience and philosophy and deserves to be quoted at length, but a summary must suffice.

After giving credit for past successes, he tries to place the hoped-for contribution of the WMS in a larger context, what they all wanted "these fellow Canadians and fellow Christians" to become. Their training in character and relationship with their culture should be rooted in home life, not an institution, "in an atmosphere of family affection and mutual helpfulness." The goal is to enhance the spiritual values in the home and its relation to school and church and community. Thus resources can be better used in encouraging and training social workers and teachers for day schools, which must be upgraded, encouraging responsibility among the young, working with them rather than for them, and so on. "The Church must revive the Indians' self-respect, their pride of accomplishment, their sense of belonging, their membership in the national fellowship on a contributory basis." When gifted youth graduate from the local school and want further technical or university training, Christian homes could be opened to them during the week, with encouragement for them to return home for weekends . . . In an address that must have lasted nearly an hour he gave them plenty to think about.

Back home he was practicing what he preached. He organized a student council which showed real initiative, not only in social events such as a weekly games night, but in a code of behaviour. Starting home and school groups took more effort. The one that served the schools on the Oneida side was a real success. The other, for the Chippewa-Muncey ones, did not fare so well. The homes were scattered; the two bands were still not well integrated. Moreover, the Bear Creek School was moved to a new location near the senior school so the same bus that brought the seniors could pick up the juniors from their isolated homes. The River Settlement School was to do the same.

At last the new senior school building was complete. Its official opening was on February 18th, 1949. It was obviously regarded by officialdom as a significant milestone in Indian education. *School News* reported that superintendents from three other reserves were present, as were the minister of Mines and Resources (which still included Indian Affairs) the Hon. Mr. MacKinnon; Major MacKay, head of that division; Mr. Emmet Morris, regional supervisor; and the Rev. George

Dorey from the Board of Home Missions, United Church. Students provided entertainment after the speeches. Of course there was an orchestra, led by Mr. Joblin with his piano accordion. The Caradoc Reserve was no longer a backwater, but front and centre.

One corner of it had always been well known because of the Mt. Elgin Residential School. By now this had been demolished—all but the original building which still housed the Joblins and another teacher, and the tall smokestack. I was interested in the way they finally brought this down without the help of dynamite. They began to remove bricks from one spot to make a notch as foresters do to cut down a tree. As they went, they shored up the hole with 4 x 4 timbers. When they were satisfied, they poured gasoline on the timbers. Helped by the chimney's draft they burned merrily. Suddenly the whole thing came down, with a crash, just where they wanted it.

Finally, in 1951, it was time to take down the original Mt. Elgin building, the one Chief Peter Jones had worked so hard to build a century before. Elgie and Helen had lived in it for four years. Now the new River Settlement School was finished and opened with some fanfare. A small apartment was attached to it. All sorts of people, young and older, gave a hand in moving the furniture over. The only thing the board provided was a kitchen stove. Elgie set up his study in the basement, complete with his old typewriter and Gestetner (the predecessors of modern computers and printers). They would live there until 1957.

XIV Some Personal Notes

Helen's mother had spent part of each winter with them. She had been lonely on the homestead since Gilbert Smith's death, and the visits were a delight to her and also to Helen; they had always been close. My own impression is that Helen was herself practically widowed by her husband's complete absorption in his work, but there is no evidence that she resented this. The modern feminist movement would take a dim view of all this, but she was brought up to believe in her lot as a homemaker and she accepted it gladly.

Mrs. Smith was about to leave for this annual visit when, on January 12th, 1949, she had a stroke. Helen went home to nurse her and stayed until September 3rd when Mrs. Smith died. Meanwhile, on May 30th, Elgie's mother died in Port Perry of a heart attack. Two sad funerals in a little over three months. Elgie had to go back to his work, so Helen had to oversee the disposition of the old homestead. It must have been very hard on her.

Within eight months Helen herself was critically ill and underwent a serious multiple operation in St. Joseph's Hospital, London. After her return to Muncey she had help for two weeks, then she was on her own again, though Elgie served as her part-time assistant. Fortunately, she made a full recovery.

I suppose this is also a "personal note" because it was not connected with his work. He had been appointed counsellor for the United Church London Conference Young Peoples' Executive. This involved meetings with them for planning programmes and events. But it also involved teaching a course at the Leadership Camp at Ryerson Beach on Lake Erie in August. Did this provide grounds for complaint in his journal? No: "It was an inspiring experience." He did it again the next year. No doubt there was a stimulating contrast between this association with young people, eager for all he could give them, and the constant effort he made back home to win a response from youth who had never had the privileged environment at home, school, and church that the youth leaders at camp enjoyed.

XV Back in Harness

It was just as well that he came back refreshed in body and spirit. New schools had been built with proper equipment; new teachers had to be "broken in"; the weekly *School News* had to be prepared and distributed. The latter job gave him a chance to do some supervising in the outlying school. He had his own class to teach, and he had to prepare for the area Track and Field Day in Mt. Brydges. At this event Muncey won three out of the four cups, a real boost for the young people's self-confidence. This time the award-giving party was held at Mt. Elgin. A note in a November issue of *School News* tells us that hot lunches were now available in the senior school—no doubt a triumph of the "Domestic Science" girls. A final edition of *School News* at the end of the school year shows that all the effort of the years 1946-51 was paying off. More students were coming, and they were staying much longer. The average age for each grade was also dropping, thanks to better schools and very little absenteeism.

XVI A Non Sequitur

At this point in the 1951 journal there is a clipping from a London newspaper that has nothing to do with the increasingly successful educational experiment except that Elgie was close enough—for once—for a family event. We have noted that brother Fred was minister at Wesley United, London. At its anniversary four ministers from one family took part. Fred conducted the service, Dad and Elgie read the lessons, and I preached. A minor weekend wonder. But something more important happened that day. Fred and Audrey had three fine boys. How they longed for a daughter! That day Anne was born—a little leaven (heaven?) in the lump of maledom. How happy Audrey was!

Other events in that busy year 1951-52 should not pass without notice. For once without a summer course, Elgie gave swimming lessons to the local children in the Thames River; there had been some near-tragedies involving non-swimmers. Then there was the planning and execution of an event that brought the Muncey ladies into a wider orbit: the Homemakers' Club Convention for Southern Ontario. The well-equipped kitchen in the senior school was a busy place. With the help of the Anglican priest, a troop of Boy Scouts and Girl Guides was organized, with permission granted to use a school bus to gather them up from far and wide. This proved to be a continuing success.

His afternoons were supposed to be free for his tasks as principal and, as superintendent, visitation of the other schools. This routine was changed for the New Year term because Mr. Johnston was absent to complete his shop training. Elgie was delighted to take his place with this "hands-on" work. He found that the older boys were bored with the artifacts prescribed by the curriculum. He had been saving plans and pictures from magazines for useful household things, and gave them their choice (one prerogative of being principal, he confided to his journal). The resulting products of free choice and initiative were gratifying. Using local walnut, they turned out a variety of useful things like small tables, which they displayed proudly in a spring show.

This year he showed the concern for the whole community that had occupied him during his eight years of ministry, but in a way unusual for a minister. He bought a 16mm movie projector and rented quality films. The charge for admission barely covered expenses, but this provided a popular social event until the arrival of TV.

He also had a continuing concern that the wider community should know more about their Indian fellow citizens. He was anxious to dispel misconceptions, so he gathered together the results of his research and experience and published them in the March '52 issue of the *Journal of the Canadian School of Psychology* under the title "The Scholastic Aptitude of the Indian Children of the Caradoc Reserve." Native intelligence did not fall short of the average; educational and reserve conditions did. When these were upgraded, so was scholastic attainment.

No doubt the most important new venture of the year besides the scouts and guides was one dear to his heart: the formation of a band. As the records show, he had gathered little groups of musicians together wherever he was. This was to be on an altogether larger scale. Using school funds he hired a Mr. A. C. Robinson to come out from London once a week. A survey of parents and pupils had suggested a positive response, but they were hardly prepared for the sixty who showed up for the first meeting. The requirements were explained: $2.00 a month for instrument rentals, $1.40 the first day for music books, regular practice at home. Fifty turned up the next week. Mr. Robinson had been able to find only forty-four used instruments. How did he match them to pupils who might not even have seen some of them? But a start was made, with enough success to merit beginning a new class the following year. Enough instruments were now available, and Elgie joined the band, learning to play the cornet. To him this was fine recreation. What did Helen think of the practicing? Let us assume he did it in the basement.

To show that this was not a failed experiment, let us "fast forward" to the records of spring 1956. Besides band concerts at home, the records show the following:

March 4:	A second concert at Wesley United
April 2:	A concert in the auditorium of the Ontario College of Education during the Ontario Education Association meeting during Easter week.
April 18:	Participation in a music festival

May 9: The Music Festival in Woodstock, where their junior group came first with eighty points.

This marked an achievement, over four years, that involved faith, hope, some charity, and no doubt much sweat and some tears.

That mention of the Ontario Education Association meetings every Easter holiday week may bring this account of 1952-53 to a satisfactory close. In 1951 a sub-section for teachers on Indian reserves was formed. In 1952 Elgie was elected president of it. There is no record in his journal of the duties this involved.

XVII An Unusual Contretemps

Music comes in minor as well as major keys. With the second band of thirty-one members, Mr. Robinson decided he could no longer be responsible for paying their rent on the instruments from the $2.00 a month paid by each member. He presented Elgie with a bill for the *purchase* of all sixty, arranged as a debt of $155.00 a month for two years. That would be quite a burden for him. But the Department of Indian Affairs, impressed by the success of this experiment also, eventually repaid him two years later.

XVIII Opportunities for Better Students

When parents and pupils were willing, Elgie encouraged bright students to go to city schools where educational opportunities were greater and where they would begin the process of integration into a culture that would be employing them later. In 1955, one was admitted to Alma College, St. Thomas, two to a business academy in London, and five to the technical school there. He discussed the possibility of apprenticeship with members of the department in London, and this led to his taking his class to meet them there. Probably the main impression with which they came away was the encouragement to stay in school as long as possible because the standards were being raised. The Muncey Senior School took students to Grade X. Eventually so many were encouraged to go further that a bus was secured to take them into London. Education had come to front and centre on the reserve.

Adult education was not entirely overlooked but had less success. In October of 1952 there was a two-week series of classes in cooking and sewing sponsored by the Women's Institute Extension. Not many older women came, though the girls from the high school class did. An evening a week for the men was a more successful venture.

XIX A Long Story with a Surprise Ending

Back in the summer of 1955 Elgie took the "Refresher Course for Elementary School Principals" and completed it successfully. It looked as though he was in for the long haul in his chosen work. But in April of '55 something happened that eventually had unforeseen results. He was appointed the secretary of a commission to study the Indian work of the United Church of Canada across the whole country. He took his first flights: on a DC3 to Toronto, then a North Star to Winnipeg. Then followed two further trips there and a final one to Toronto, on April 13th and 14th. Then he had to pull all the reports and discussions together in a report to General Council in the fall. All this with no letup in his educational programme.

His work on the commission made him realize that he did not know at firsthand the far-flung work of the church among its Indians. So he planned a working holiday for the summer, visiting as many as possible. He bought a small 8 x 8 tent and some camping equipment—and invited Helen to come along. This she did, no doubt with misgivings, but thinking she would just be going to Northern Ontario. Her hopeful husband did not tell her of his larger plans until he found out how well she was taking to camping. When it came time to turn west he introduced the subject. There is no record of the debate, but the affirmative won, and Helen went along. At least she had her husband to herself for a change.

There is no time to tell of the vicissitudes of the long northern route, visiting reserves, crawling through stretches of repair work, having the flywheel housing dented by a rock, coping with black flies. In the Prairie Provinces the going was better. They visited some residential schools that were still in operation, where the welcome was warm and the tent unneeded. Finally they made it to Edmonton, to Calgary and the Stoney Reserve, and headed for home, still, I trust, speaking to each other.

After getting the school year started on the home front, Elgie headed for Windsor where he gave his report to the General Council on

September 19th. The *Observer* called it a very good report. The *Christian Century* said: "The report is a perceptive analysis which deserves to be studied by everyone who is concerned with racial justice and Christian Service."

But the story told in the Canadian press was different and caused anger and much distress. It misquoted the report, and in summing it up was grievously erroneous. It printed a retraction, but the damage had been done as radio and press took up the story. It reminds me of the tale of a malicious gossip who made her confession to the priest. "Your penance is in two parts," said the good Father. "You must take a feather pillow out on the street, and remove its stuffing there. Then come back to me." She did so and returned. "Now go back and pick up all the feathers." "But Father, the wind blew them everywhere!" "Just so. You told me you were sorry about your false gossip. What are you going to do about the damage you have done?"

The misquote used the words "excessive laziness" instead of "excessive idleness," and "lack of personal initiative" instead of "lack of personal incentive and community endeavour." The false summary said the United Church described most Canadian reserve Indians as "lazy, immoral, non-social, and unambitious."

Let me quote Elgie's reaction as written in his journal:

> As the one who read the report as Secretary, the full weight of Indians' displeasure fell on me, and I was devastated, heart-broken. Known quite widely among the Indians after 24 years of work with them, and 10 years as publisher of *Wampum*, it came as a cruel blow to many Indian friends, for of course they believed what they read and heard, false though it was . . . It was obvious to me that my position at Muncey must be relinquished.

He told no one about this at the time, because the work of the school year had to go on. And go on it did, all the organizations flourishing, and a new one started, Teen Town. The band was in its glory, as "goodwill ambassadors." They won the cup at the Woodstock Festival. The school year ended with a flourish, an open-air band concert. But it did not lessen his resolve. "Last year's experience had taken the heart out of me, had destroyed a relationship that had taken me over twenty years to nurture . . . It was time to leave." This was the last entry in his Muncey journal. It could not have been as bad as he thought. But *he* thought it was. And that mattered.

When we were young, we had a board game called "Snakes and Ladders." By tossing the dice you climbed a ladder, sometimes by one or two rungs, until you reached the top and achieved your goal. But at any point you might land on a snake's mouth and slide down to a lower rung. There was even a snake near the top that could send you back to the bottom, and effectively put you out of the game. Elgie must have felt he had stepped on that snake.

Perhaps the goal he missed planning was the last in the ladder of new schools for the Indians on the Caradoc Reserve, dedicated June 3rd, 1960. It was the fifth in the series he had begun and contained six rooms including a "gymtorium." It cost a quarter of a million dollars. The usual representatives from the government and education were there to speak, as were the chiefs of the three bands: Oneida, Chippewa, and Muncey. And—praise be—they asked Elgie back as the final speaker. That must have been balm to his soul.

Three hundred and fifty pupils were expected the following year. He pointed out that this had nothing to do with a higher birthrate, but everything to do with the quality of education they could now receive on the reserve. Some families had returned from the towns to which they had gone so their children could be better educated. But most of the increase was due to a decrease in dropouts. Even the slow learners felt welcome in the auxiliary class, where they could discover their latent potentialities. He had his reward.

Now, before we see him start to climb another ladder, let us return to his decision to leave the game he had enjoyed so much. Here, quoted in full, are his letter of resignation, and the one that shows the reaction of the authorities:

* * *

MT. ELGIN INDIAN DAY SCHOOL
Muncey, Ontario.

March 2, 1957

Mr. R. F. Davey,
Education Division,
Indian Affairs Branch,
Citizenship and Immigration,
Ottawa, Ontario.

Dear Mr. Davey,

During this school year, it has become quite clear that in the best interests of the work at Caradoc, it is time for me to resign my position and leave the way clear for someone else to take over the work. Please accept this letter as my resignation, to take effect June 30th.

My own decision was made last October, but in the hope of avoiding harmful repercussions during the year, I thought it best to delay announcing my plans. Even now, I would prefer that the fact should not become known locally, but in order that you and Mr. Mingay might have a fair chance of making suitable arrangements for a successor, I feel compelled to risk the premature publicity.

It would be unwise for me to attempt an explanation within the limits of this letter, but I should be quite willing to discuss the matter with you at some future date, if the best interests of the work would be served thereby. In the meantime, I intend to inform no-one locally of my plans, nor to enter into discussion on the subject. It is my hope that the change can be made without harmful effects to the work itself or to the Indian Affairs Branch and its officials. For local consumption, it is just "time for a change." I have done what I set out to do, and from this point on, I believe another can do what should be done better than I could do it.

I should like to thank you sincerely for your co-operation and support during the years of our association, and for the opportunity I have had for serving the Indian people.

Copies to:
Mr. H. G. Mingay
Rev. M. C. Macdonald

Respectively Yours,

E. E. M. Joblin

* * *

PERSONAL & CONFIDENTIAL

Toronto, Ontario.
March 18, 1957

Indian Affairs Branch,
Ottawa, Ontario.

Attention: Mr. R. F. Davey,

Re: E. M. Joblin, M.A.
Supervising Principal,
Caradoc Indian Agency

Undoubtedly you were rather disturbed, as I surely was, to receive a resignation from Mr. Joblin. I had intended to spend a week at Caradoc for some time and consequently I went to Caradoc and spent the whole of the week of March 11th on the reserve. I could easily put in another week on the reserve, and I am planning to do this before the end of May.

If Mr. Joblin were from the North we might use the term "bushed" to describe Mr. Joblin's condition. He has spent twenty-one years on the reserve and given the best of his life to these people. His efforts have by no means been wasted. A great many of these people, and the younger people in particular, have advanced in a very accelerated manner, largely due to Mr. Joblin's efforts. The situation in the outlying schools is excellent (Grades one to six). I would say that with the exception of Bear Creek most of the schools are doing very good work. Where, however, the adolescents are congregated at Mount Elgin, discipline is not too good and I feel that to a marked extent Mr. Joblin has been doing the work single-handed. He has not had the type of teachers that would give him the support he needs, and he has not had a principal in this school. I do not think the teen-age problem at Muncey is too far out of line with the teen-age problem in many provincial centres. The adolescent poses a very marked problem in the work of education today. Unless one has competent, sympathetic teachers, teenagers are always a problem.

Most of the teachers leave the school fairly promptly at the close of the day. Mr. Joblin, however, resident as he is at the school, puts in a very long day, not only on school days, but is there Saturdays and Sundays, and in the main the people respect his judgment, his advice, and there is usually some parent at the residence talking things over with him no matter when one visits the school. We have not been able to get a good principal at Mount Elgin and consequently Mr. Joblin does the work of local principal as well as supervising principal. He has been the motivating force behind the Guides, Scouts, and Cubs, the band and the Parent-Teachers Associations, of which there are two. He publishes a newsletter weekly which recapitulates the activities of the various organizations on the reserve, and of course which promotes very markedly the work of the schools and the achievements of the children.

Mr. Joblin has effected an excellent liaison between his schools and pupils, with the London Board of Education and the Business Colleges in London. The Board of Education in London and the Provincial Inspectors have every respect for his judgment and his work. In view of these circumstances it would be very regrettable if Mr. Joblin should be allowed to pass out of the picture.

One thing is certain, he should be off the reserve, and he himself feels this. I do not think he and Mrs. Joblin have had a reasonable holiday since they began their work at Muncey. They very rarely go to a concert or anything out at London or Chatham because most of his evenings during the week are taken up with band practice, teachers meetings, Cubs, Scouts, Guides, as I have mentioned.

I had lunch with Mr. and Mrs. Joblin one day and talked over the situation with them. He tells me that he has made no plans for the future and that he has not advised the Church that he is available for duty in a pastoral or executive position. This means that he is still in a position to serve the Branch.

I suggested to him that he live in London or Chatham and continue as supervising principal at Muncey, and also take in the supervisory duties at Moraviantown, Walpole Island and Kettle Point. This arrangement could very well be effected if he were resident at Chatham or London. He also has in mind the possibility of a year's leave of absence to finish his doctorate. His M.A., as you are aware, was done in education and is the equivalent of a B.Paed. He chose to take the master's degree rather than the B.Paed., when the degree was granted. He has done one year's work in education in advance of this and has another year and a thesis to prepare to receive his Ph.D., or a doctorate in education. He thought he might do this next year and it would give him an opportunity to visit a good many provincial schools and reassure himself with regard to standards. I felt sure you would like to know about these two plans.

Mr. Joblin proposes to come into Ottawa to see you and Mr. Morris, and Mr. Bonnah, and I hope that you will be able to prevail upon him to remain in the service.

H. G. Mingay,
Inspector of Schools

HGM:lb
c.c. Mr. Joblin

* * *

Third Movement

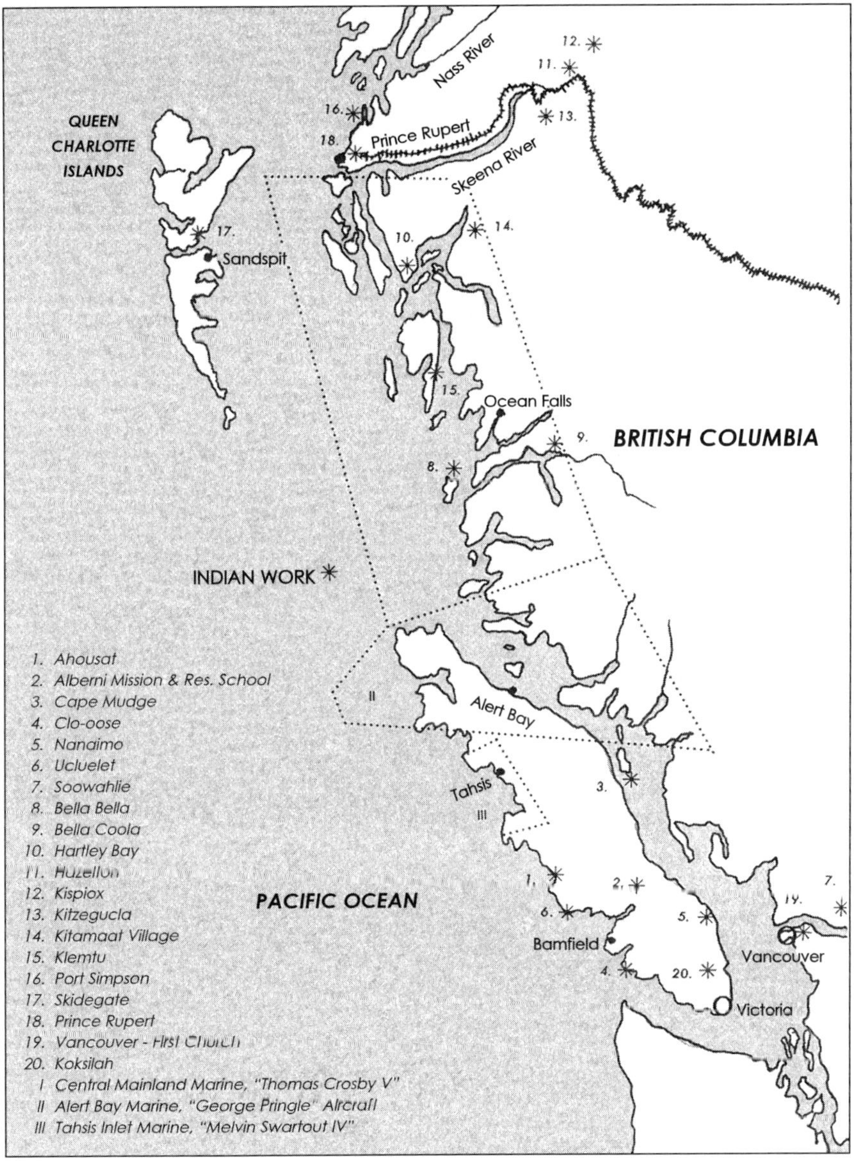

3. Indian Work and Marine Missions in British Columbia

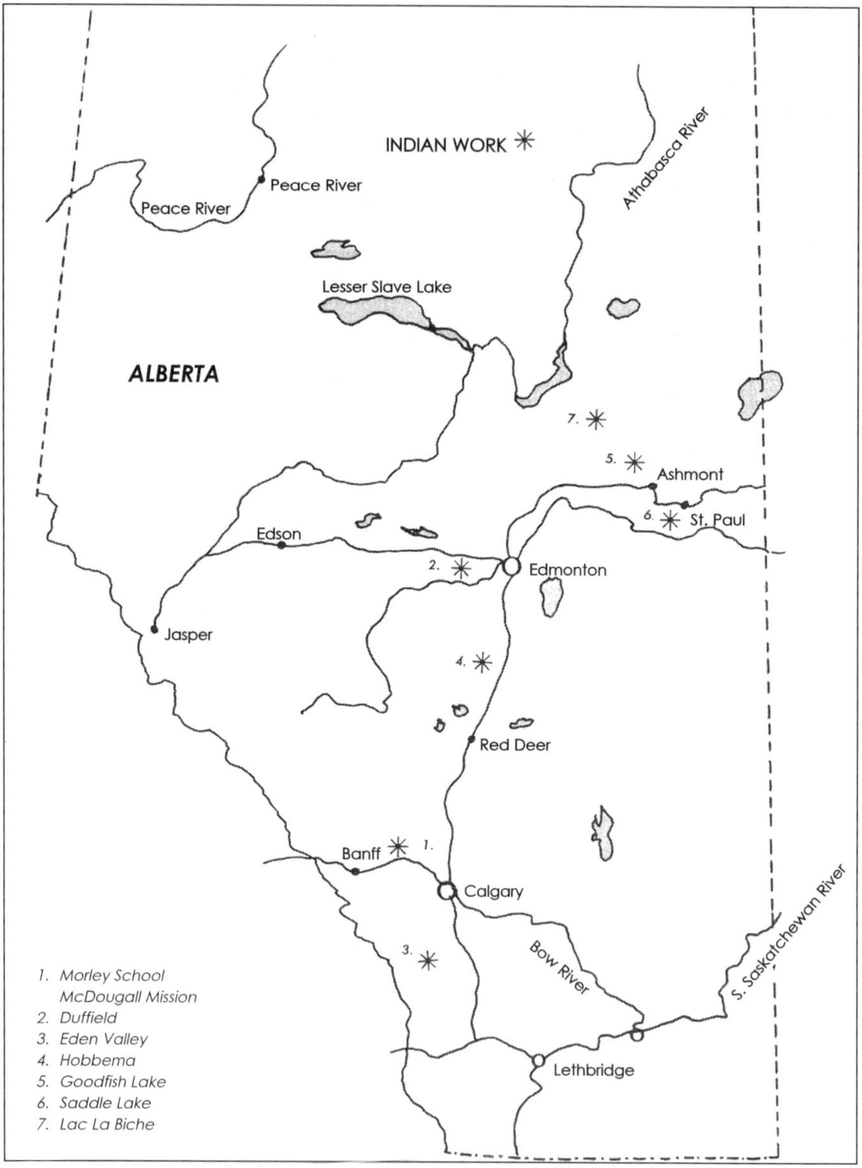

4. Indian Work in Alberta

The Elgie family visits the Joblin manse at Melrose. Dad's hand rests on little Elgie's head. (p. 11)

One of Dad's rural churches (Mt. Pleasant) where Elgie was recommended for the Ministry, 1928. (p. 18)

One of the churches on the Cordova Mines charge where Elgie served as a probationer, 1928-30. (p. 19)

Curve Lake Indian Congregation, 1935. (p. 22)

Arts Graduation, 1933. (p. 23)

The cottage on Buckhorn Lake, built from recycled logs (Wesley United Church, including Curve Lake Mission, 1933-36). (p. 24)

Muncey "Mission House" where Elgie and Helen lived, 1936-44. (p. 37)

How Elgie transported ball teams and Sunday school children, 1936-44. (p. 38)

The congregation of Central Church, Oneida, 1940. (p. 38)

Formed from the two Oneida frame churches, built by Uncle Fred Elgie with volunteer Indian labour. (pp. 39-40)

The original Mt. Elgin (1849). Elgie and Helen lived upstairs for four years. (p. 56)

The multipurpose new school basement. (p. 60)

"Mt. Elgin," Muncey, closed 1948. (p. 61)

A manual training class taught by Elgie. (p. 64)

The band at one of the new schools replacing the residential school. (p. 65)

An Indian wedding, 1950.

In his office, 1968. (p. 85)

Norway House day school class. (pp. 91-93)

At Norway House, 1957, with an Indian lady, over 90 years of age. (p. 93)

A 27-mile trip to Deer Lake, Northern Ontario, 1962. Elgie is end man on the sleigh. (p. 98)

Leather plaque given to Elgie after working all night with the Indians to ready the church and hall for opening. (p. 98)

1959 GRADUATION CLASS — ALBERNI INDIAN RESIDENTIAL SCHOOL 1959

L. to R. (Back Row)—Bill Jones, Charles Coon, Richard Atleo

L. to R. (Front Row)—Sylvia Saunders, Sophinia Wallace, Donna Sepass, Mary Smart

Graduation class, Alberni Indian Residential School, 1959. (pp. 102-103)

Elgie helps dedicate the first United Church plane, based at Alert Bay, B.C., 1960. (p. 103)

Dual purpose church/hall, Moose Mt. Reserve, Saskatchewan, 1960.

Aspen Cove, Newfoundland, 1961. Built by volunteer labour. (p. 108)

United Church House, H.Q. for Elgie on the Board of Home Missions, 1957-70. (p. 110)

YES, THE HAIR IS THEIR OWN

"The Chieftones," Canada's all Indian band,—the new sensation among the younger set. The band plays Rock 'N Roll, Rhythm and Blues, Folk, Western, and Religious Music. They have traveled thousands of miles throughout Canada and the States, have made many TV appearances, and have made many friends. In the group are Jack Cecil, a Niska; Albert Canadien, a Slave; Richard Douse, and brothers Barry and Vincent Clifford, Gitksan Indians.

The Chieftones were formed in Edmonton, Alberta, in 1964. U.C. Residential School

The Chieftones, Canada's all-Indian band, were formed in a United Church Residential School in Edmonton, Alberta, in 1964.

Four senior girls from the Home Economics class, with dresses they made.

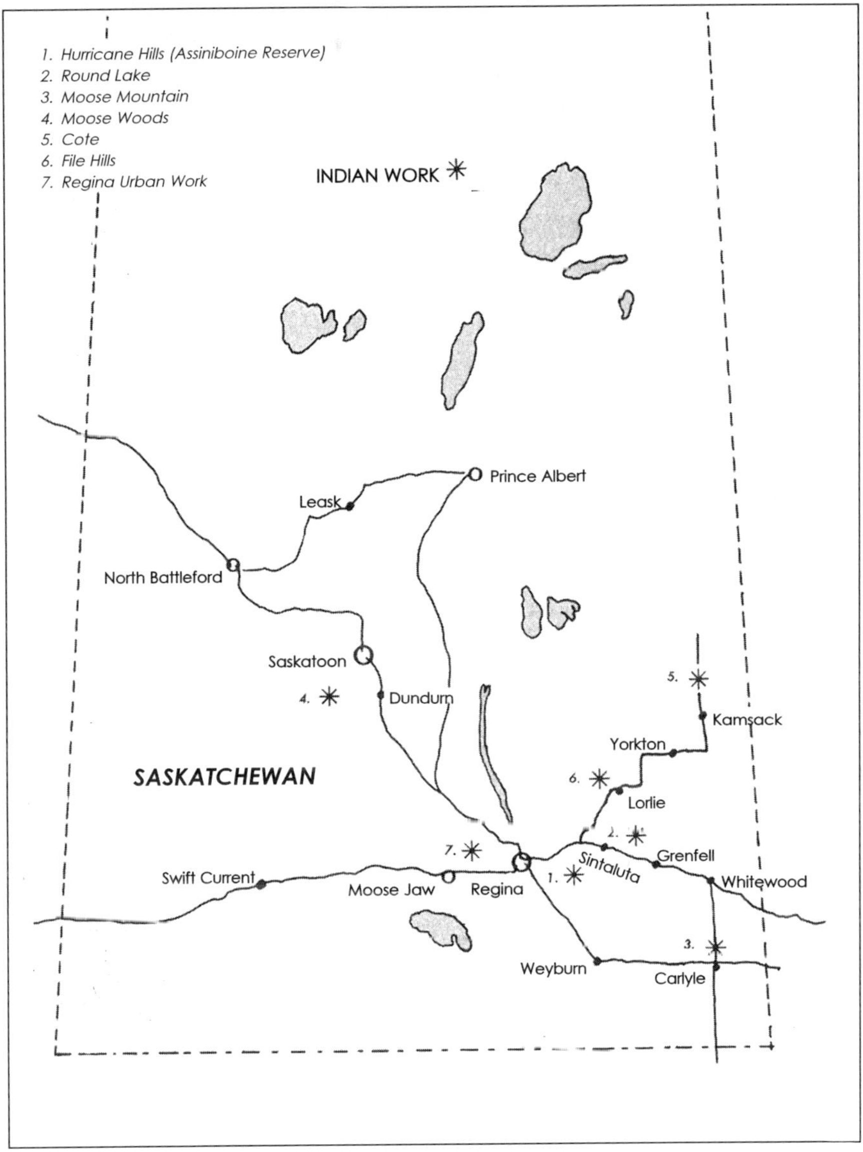

5. Indian Work in Saskatchewan

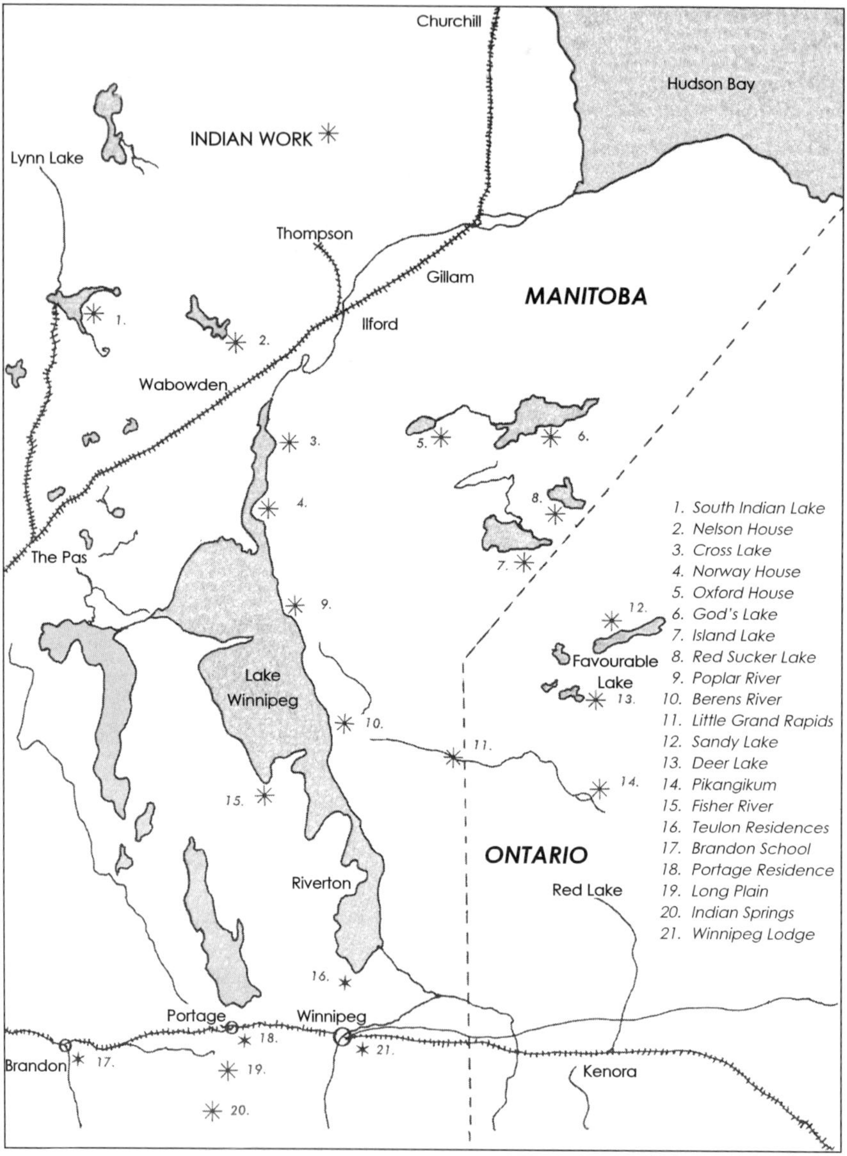

6. Indian Work in Manitoba

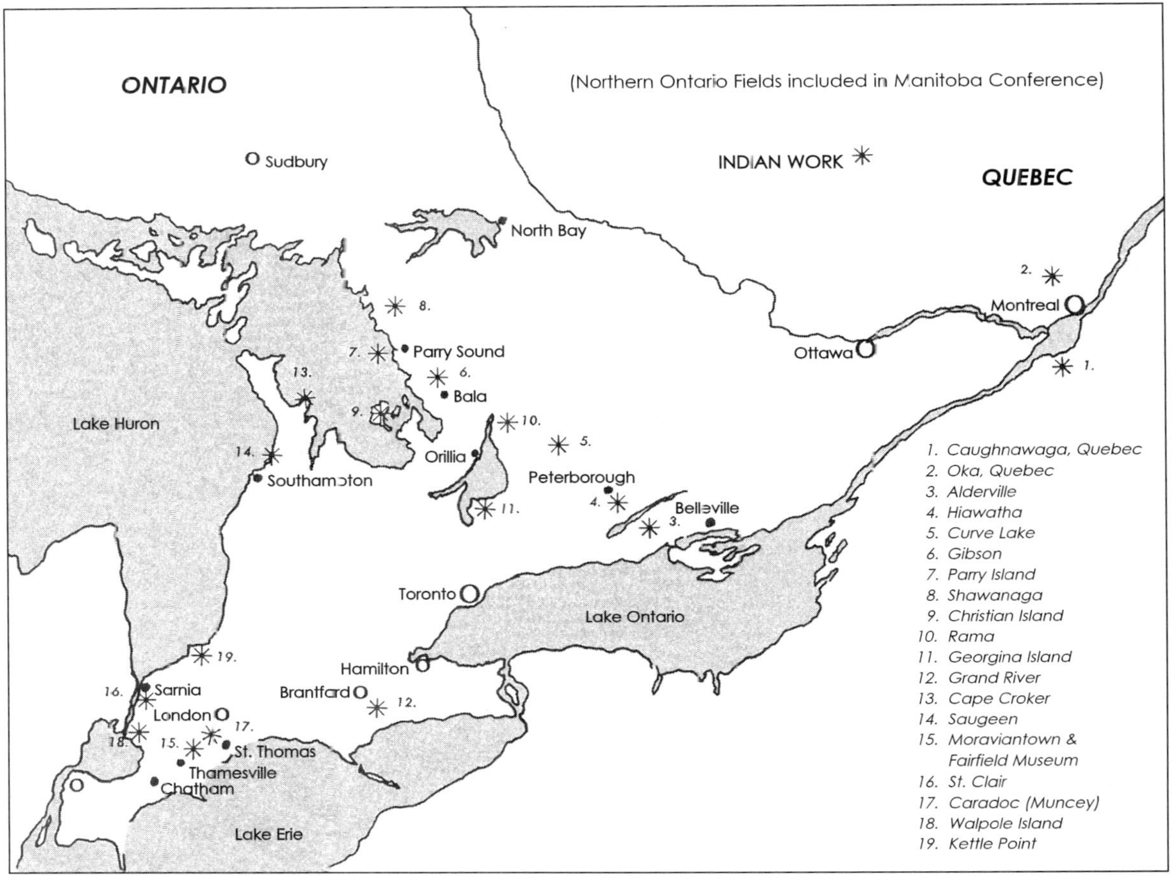

7. Indian Work in Ontario and Quebec

Theme: Serving First Nations from Sea to Sea

XX "Wider, Still Wider, Shall Thy Bounds Be Set"

Elgie's title in his journal was not so bombastic: "Another Chapter, Another Move, Another Sphere of Action." He may have been looking forward to a needed rest and a quiet year of study finishing his doctorate. "Man proposes, God disposes." There is no doubt that it was God who was disposing. The final assembly at the Mt. Elgin School was on Friday, June 28th, 1957. His new position stated that it began on July 1st. He was in his new office on the second.

His resignation started a flurry of activity in Ottawa and Toronto. At that Windsor General Council, and as a result of the maligned commission of which Elgie was a member, it had been decided that the church's Indian work must receive more attention. Large bodies are supposed to move ponderously. But when the Home Mission Board heard that the Indian Affairs Department was about to offer their prize educationist an important position, they acted immediately. They offered Elgie the job of assistant secretary of the board, with his main responsibility the oversight of all its Indian work from Atlantic to Pacific. He accepted. He gave his new job his "best shot" for the next fourteen years.

This was a new position, and the board worked out carefully what would now be described as a job description. I quote here one page of the rather daunting "Memorandum":

MEMORANDUM RE: The Administration of Our Indian Work

Following the study and recommendations of the Commission on Indian Work, the Board of Home Missions requested the appointment to the Home Mission office of the Secretary who could give general administration to our Church's work among the Indian people. As a result, Rev. E. E. M. Joblin was appointed Assistant Secretary and began his duties July 1st, 1957. The major portion of Mr. Joblin's time is devoted to the various phases of Home Mission services among our Indian constituencies.

Terms of Reference of Mr. Joblin's office:

1. He is general supervisor, in consultation and co-operation with the Superintendents of Missions, of all Indian work of The United Church of Canada. This work can be divided roughly into three main types, namely, missionary work on pastoral charges, the work in various types of schools, and work among Indian people in our towns and cities.

2. He is responsible for formulating and recommending to the Board of Home Missions the policy to be followed in carrying out our responsibility to our Indian constituencies.

3. He represents the Board of Home Missions in any approaches that must be made to the Indian Affairs Branch and its various services in Ottawa. Further, in the working out of any policies or recommendations arising out of such conferences with the Department in Ottawa, he consults and co-operates with the Superintendents of Missions in their application at the Presbytery level.

4. He is responsible for outlining to the Board of Home Missions and its Executive the programme of property rehabilitation and estimates in the various Presbyteries where Indian work occurs. In the formulating of such a programme and estimates he confers with the Superintendent of Missions and the Presbytery concerned.

5. A very special responsibility and concern is the administration of our residential schools, including the nominating of the principals, negotiations between the Principal and government officials in the operation of the school and the appropriations required for its operation, property rehabilitation, and adequate provision of school facilities for all Indian youth for whom the United Church is responsible.

6. The initiation of new forms of service among Indian folk who migrate to our cities, such as hostels, service centres, and programmes for the integration of Indian youth into the life and work of the Church.

Relationship of the Superintendent to this Programme:

In all of the above, care has been taken to emphasize the necessity for the closest possible co-operation between Mr. Joblin and the Superintendents. The responsibilities should be shared, not divided between them. As far as possible, all matters will be brought to the attention of Mr. Joblin and the Board through the usual channels, such as the Home Mission Committee, the Presbytery and the Superintendent. When there is occasion for direct correspondence, copies should be sent to the office of the Superintendent.

But first Elgie had to move to a second-floor apartment on Highbourne Road. The van arrived on Tuesday, July 2nd. Elgie was not there, but in his new office. This was surely not premeditated! But Helen was in charge of the move, and her sister and brother-in-law Osbourne had been recruited. That was fortunate. Elgie had given Helen a cheque for the agreed amount, but the movers would not accept it because it had not been certified. No money, no furniture. Somehow Osbourne made it up, and when Elgie came home everything was in place.

He may have gotten off lightly on moving day, but he did not spare himself in his work. One of the first things he wanted to do was visit the places and people for whom he was now responsible. A careful evaluation of the quality of the work and an assessment of available equipment were needed. Yet he believed it was most important to establish personal relations with the workers and to assure them that "Head Office" was behind them. July was devoted to correspondence and planning, and to some visits in Ontario. From August 14th to October 6th he was on the road (or in the air) from Manitoba to British Columbia. The strenuousness of this trip can be inferred from a summary that prefaced the full report he submitted when he returned. We will transcribe two-thirds of it here. It will be noted that many of the trips to reserves in Manitoba and the majority in B.C. were by boat. These included voyages aboard the *Thomas Crosby IV*, the last in a line of famous missionary ships that took the minister/skipper to the coastal villages:

Itinerary, August 14 - October 6, 1957

Rev. E. E. M. Joblin

Aug. 14-15	*Toronto - Winnipeg (Canadian, 4:15 p.m. - 10:20 p.m.) Stayed overnight with Dr. McMillan*
Aug. 16	*To Lac Du Bonnet (2 hrs.) "Transair" to Island Lake. Visited Mr. and Mrs. Tom Hamilton until noon next day.*
Aug. 17	*Left Island Lake at noon, arrived Norway House School 3:30 p.m. Assisted in Bible School from time of arrival until Friday morning, Aug. 23. Preached Sunday and Wednesday evening.*
Aug. 23	*Norway House to Winnipeg—stopping at Oxford House, Gods' Mine, God's Lake, Red Sucker Lake (picked up Jack Witty), Island Lake and Little Grand Rapids (picked up Mr. Watson). Reached Winnipeg 8:30 p.m.*
Aug. 24	*Morning with Dr. McMillan. Afternoon took bus for Swan Lake. Spent week-end with Rev. and Mrs. Matthews.*
Aug. 25	*Spoke at three services - Swan Lake, Altamont, Indian Springs (Indian). Visited several families.*
Aug. 26	*Left 8:30 a.m. to visit Long Plain (Matthew driving). Mr. Buhr, single, student. On to Portage La Prairie Res. School. Caught bus at 5 p.m. for Winnipeg. Evening for making notes.*
Aug. 27	*Morning with Dr. McMillan. Indian Affairs offices. Afternoon - interviewed Mr. and Mrs. Lyman (Fisher River)—on to Teulon—visited schools and Cameron Reid.* *Evening - visited Mr. and Mrs. Graham (Oxford House)*

and caught Train for Regina.

Aug. 28	*Arrived Regina 10:15 a.m. - Mr. Stade took me to see Zion church—lunch and visit with Mr. Mackenzie (on Commission). Caught T.C.A. plane for Edmonton. Reached Res. School in time for supper.*
Aug. 29	*Morning with Indian Affairs officials; afternoon Lamont Hospital, evening with Dr. Woodsworth.*
Aug. 30	*Morning with officials and Rev. Dwight Powell; Afternoon to Duffield Mission. Supper and evening at Bissell Church Camp.*
Aug. 31	*Met Rev. & Mrs. Morgan at Beulah Home & drove with them to Ashmont, arriving 4 p.m., for week-end.*
Sept. 1	*All day going to Goodfish Lake and back. Baptized Morgan's newly-adopted daughter. Caught bus for Edmonton 7 p.m., arrived at School 1:30 a.m.*
Sept. 2	*Met Mr. Powell for trip to Hobbema Reserve. Back to the School for supper and a thorough inspection of the School and Farm, along with Mr. Powell.*
Sept. 3	*Spent morning on reports. Caught train for Hazelton 3 p.m.*
Sept. 4	*En route. Reached Hazelton in time for supper. Evening in Bible Study group at Hospital.*
Sept. 5	*Morning at Kitzegucla, afternoon at Kispiox, evening with McIntoshes.*
Sept. 6	*Chapel Service at Hospital; afternoon at Hospital. Took train for Prince Rupert.*
Sept. 7	*Prince Rupert to Sandspit (air), to Skidegate (bus and*

boat); afternoon in Indian village; evening with Dr. Bowyer.

Sept. 8	*Took 3 services, Charlotte City, Sandspit and Skidegate.*
Sept. 9	*Took all morning to get back to Prince Rupert. Met by Rev. Oliver Howard and "Thomas Crosby IV". Interview with Dr. Fiddes and Mr. Hubert Deardon. Left for Port Simpson about 2:50 p.m., arrived 5:30 p.m. Spent evening at Port Simpson,—service at church.*
Sept. 10	*Left 4 a.m. for Hartley Bay, arriving 4:15 p.m. Spent evening and overnight there.*
Sept. 11	*Took morning to reach Kitamat (new). Visited Rev. Ross Connal and saw townsite. Took him with us for visit to Kitamat Indian Village. Stayed for evening service and visit with teachers. Took Mr. Connal back and docked for night.*
Sept. 12	*All day to reach Klemtu (6:20 p.m.) Evening services in the church (Wm. Robinson and Louis Clifton).*
Sept. 13	*Started for Bella Bella, stopping at Ivory Island lighthouse. Reached Bella Bella 7:20 p.m. for week-end. Evening with staff.*
Sept. 14	*Reached Ocean Falls 9:30 a.m.; remained until 9:20 p.m. Arrived Bella Coola 7:20 p.m. for week-end. Evening with staff.*
Sept. 15	*Sunday - Spoke at morning & evening services, and S.S. in afternoon. Song service after church at doctor's residence.*
Sept. 16	*Left for Namu to connect with steamship. Spent afternoon and night there. Met summer student.*

Sept. 17 *Expected steamer at 4 a.m.—arrived 5:15. Arrived Alert Bay 5:15 p.m.*

Sept. 18 *Spent day at Alert Bay. Could not get plane earlier.*

Sept. 19 *Alert Bay - Cape Mudge, via Port Hardy, Comox, Campbell River. Arrived 3:30 p.m. Remained until 10 p.m. Visit at hotel (Campbell R.) with Rev. E. S. Fleming.*

Sept. 20 *Campbell River by bus to Nanaimo. Afternoon with Dr. & Mrs. Kelly at Parksville. Mr. Caldwell picked me up at 4:30—reached Alberni school for supper & evening.*

Sept. 21 *Plane for Ahousat—reached there at noon. Remained for afternoon, evening, all night.*

Sept. 22 *Spoke at morning service. Plane back to Alberni (5:30 p.m.). Showed pictures to pupils in evening.*

Sept. 23 *At Alberni school until noon. Mr. Caldwell drove me to Nanaimo. Evening at Nanaimo Indian Church with Dr. Kelly. Spoke to officials.*

I would also like to include a sample of the reports that he made in point form about every place he visited. This one concerns Norway House in Northern Manitoba. He must have been pleased to visit it because Dad had taught there at the beginning of the century, and his diary had been full of interesting narratives.

MEMO: RE NORWAY HOUSE - NORWAY HOUSE MISSION

Rev. Reg. Brown, unmarried, starting second year.
Visited Aug. 17-23, 1957 (Bible School).

Manse - *Frame house, equipped with water supply and electric power from central supply. Modern plumbing. Furnishings, mostly adequate, include new stove and refrigerator.*

Criticism: Work needed on interior—tape over joints of wallboard is peeling off. Redecorating needed. Plumbing freezes up (against outside wall). Water supply froze up last year and thawed out third week of August. House is cold, in spite of large wood furnace and large supplies of 3-foot wood. Power mower would be valuable for manse and church.

Church - In excellent condition, well furnished, attractive and in commanding position. The strategic centre of our work in Northern Manitoba.

Schools - Residential: new, modern in every way. Principal, Mr. John Dennys (wife and two small boys). In good hands. Amply supplied with Christmas gifts.
Day School: modern, 3-room, now under principalship of Mr. Dennys.
Educational needs: well provided for—if sufficient staff provided.

Hall - Near church, used by other organizations but under control of our church. Not large, but useful.

Other Buildings - Shed and boathouse shared with Residential School. Adequate.

Transportation - Minister has own boat, second hand but adequate - ($75).

Personnel - Rev. Brown, capable, doing good work and has respect of the people. However, due to unmarried status, is anxious to leave. Concur in this—as soon as replacement is found.

General - A key position, requiring person of experience and tact, a co-ordinator of all the services. Big challenge for the right people.

The reference to the historic residential school at Norway House reminds us of Elgie's position in regard to them: only under exceptional situations should children be removed from their homes and put into such "foreign" environments. The United Church still operated six such schools on the Prairies and in B.C. He tried to visit each one every year. Did they still justify their existence? This was long before any breath of scandal had touched these institutions. Were there pupils there who could live with their parents and siblings while going to day schools? If there were none near them, could they board with Indian families or sympathetic white families and go home on weekends?

The fact was that there were many "exceptional situations," especially in thinly populated areas of Western Canada. Most Indians wanted their children to get some education. Where no day schools existed, or where transportation was difficult or dangerous (e.g., by water), there was a need for these schools, and there were orphans and problem children who could be cared for and rehabilitated there. Elgie believed that every youth should have the choice of whether to seek integration with the dominant society or continue in his/her inherited culture. But to make this choice they needed at least an introduction through education to the technical culture at their doorstep. This did not mean that the residential school should ignore their age-old culture and spirituality, as had been the case historically. Shouldn't they be introduced to their own tribal history? And encouraged to use their own language? He had done both in Muncey. The ideal would be to have teachers from their own race—this was Chief Peter Jones' hope for Mt. Elgin 100 years ago. It would take a lot of effort and encouragement to make such dreams come true.

And much as he admired the dedication of the missionaries on the reserves, why couldn't more Indians be trained for this ministry? (He would live to see a real beginning in this.) Back at Muncey he had encouraged the elders to conduct their prayer meetings in their own languages. Now he was seeing how some of them took over the work of an absent missionary, and how others worshipped from their Cree bibles and hymn books in remote areas. There was hope.

XXI Communicating

While in Muncey Elgie had made communication with colleagues a priority: ten years with *Wampum*, eleven with *School News*. He had found it invaluable for morale as well as shared information. He launched the same policy now, beginning with a weighty *Manual*. It started with information, first on the relation of the Ottawa bureaucracy (then called the Department of Citizenship and Immigration) under H. M. Jones and the regional offices in the provinces; then the organization of the United Church in its relation to workers in the field, in pastoral charges, schools, and hospitals. For the smooth operation of their work and a speedy solution of their problems these people, on whom the whole operation depended, should know who was responsible for what. So the manual explains the "chain of command": the Board of Home Missions with its specific secretary and its area superintendents; the conference that recommends grants; the local presbyteries and their Home Mission committees. There follow three articles by Elgie covering educational policy, relations with community agencies, and preparation of the workers for their jobs.

Then he gets down to the main purpose of the *Manual*: inspiration and practical advice. Article after article, by acknowledged leaders in various aspects of the work like the legendary Dr. George Darby of the B.C. coastal missions, tell of their understanding of the aborigines, their methods, successes, and suggestions. So the *Manual* reminds me of the cartoon about the rooster who found an ostrich egg and called the hens around: "Ladies, I don't want to complain, but see what others are doing!"

There were quarterly supplements to this original issue, and the workers were encouraged to put these into a binder that was provided. When leaving their position, they were asked to leave this behind as a sourcebook for their successors. To Elgie's dismay, there must have been a fairly large turnover. In the first issue for September 1961, there is a cheery welcome to sixteen new recruits (see Appendix I).

Every now and then he also sent out a two-page letter of clever or encouraging quotations gleaned from his reading, along with bibliographies and comments on helpful books. He must have kept his secretary busy. I wonder if she ever compared notes with Helen? For example, he found two passages he thought important in a book by E. A. Nida: *Customs and Cultures—Anthropology of Christian Missions:*

> p. 91: One of the major contrasts between Western secularized culture (in which religion is only for Sunday) and most primitive cultures is the high degree in which in primitive societies religion pervades all aspects of life. These cultures are now undergoing drastic upheavals, in which the spiritual values are being violently denied or indifferently cast aside. The Christian missionary can potentially be one of the greatest integrating forces in the present cultural turmoil and change, if in the conflict produced by the new technologies he can show the complete relevance of his life-embracing message.
>
> p. 140: Another feature of our analysis is the avoidance of the weighted word "superstition." It is too easy to miss some important resemblance by passing off other peoples' beliefs as "superstitions" and regarding one's own as "doctrines." In the same way that we would avoid "savage" and "native" when talking about social and material culture, we do well to avoid the word "superstition" in talking of religion.

XXII A Three-Ringed Circus?

If his work had been confined to his chief responsibility he might have had time for some home life and shared cultural activities, especially his fondness for music, with Helen. But he had to take his share of the board's responsibilities in other aspects of the church's life. It looks like a lion's share, since he was the junior member, though probably it was not. Here are some of the committees to which he was posted:

The Rural Life Committee
The United Church Training School
The Church Extension Committee
The Missionary Education Committee
The National Committee on the Canadian Indian
The Canadian Churches' Forum for Global Ministries
The Canadian School of Missions, later called
  The Ecumenical Institute

The last of these eventually asked him to be chairman of the board. As such he took part in many planning sessions with its secretary, Canon Jim Puxley. They became close friends. On Elgie's retirement he presented him with J. H. Oldham's *Devotional Diary*, with a Latin inscription and "with abiding affection."

For one five-week period in the winter of '67 I counted twelve meetings, four of them out of the city, such as a trip to assess the work at Caughnawaga and Oka, during which he also preached at each place. Our sister Gladys had taught in the Protestant School in Caughnawaga, so this visit had a personal interest.

He resolved that he needed to involve the conferences and local presbyteries in more responsibility for the Indian work in their areas. This meant more work to him, and not only when visiting them. The Kenora-Rainy River Presbytery took its work seriously—and asked him to investigate the situation in the North. So with two of their ministers he chartered a Norseman plane and went to Pikangikum, Deer Lake, and Sandy Lake. Work on buildings was authorized at each place. Eventually a return trip was made to dedicate the resulting new structures. This time the main stop was at Sandy Lake, where he dedicated a new manse as well as a new church. The presbytery group had chartered a small Norseman. But a large delegation from Winnipeg who wanted to share the celebration had come in a flying boat. The church was full; the visitors had to stand in the back. The service was almost entirely in Cree. The Indians do not like to hurry their hymns. One lady from Winnipeg told Elgie that she had come to the end of a verse only to find that the Cree singers were halfway through. The visitors had thoughtfully brought food, and proceeded to cook their hot dogs over a campfire. They discovered that the Indians had not done so. Those who had come from afar stood around, looking on hungrily. The food was shared, but there was no multiplication of wieners and buns.

He spent the evening visiting the young teacher and his wife. Their home was tiny; he slept on the kitchen floor. He had a pleasant surprise the next day when they flew to Deer Lake. The teacher was an old friend from the Chippewa Reserve at Muncey, Mrs. Mina Robinson. It was a happy reunion. At Pikangikum there was a service in *their* new church. And finally he went back to Red Lake. It took all of the following day to drive back to Winnipeg with the Rev. N. K. Campbell, the superintendent for Home Missions in Manitoba. There was plenty of time for consultation.

After a visit to Norway House during the week, he "hitched a ride" in a two-seater plane to Berens River on Lake Winnipeg for another new church dedication. It was Saturday afternoon, and chaos reigned. The cleaning up had only just started, and a large delegation of visitors was expected for the Sunday service. Elgie borrowed coveralls from the minister and they worked all night. Everybody seemed to enjoy the situation. As a thank you to Elgie they gave him a small but beautiful leather hanging with fine beadwork.

In working with his hands here, as in the earlier episode of helping build the Oneida Church, he was unconsciously fulfilling a qualification for a missionary to the Indians stipulated 100 years earlier by Peter Jones. The first ordained minister to the Credit River Reserve, Egerton Ryerson, had rolled up his sleeves and worked alongside his parishioners. Peter Jones wrote this:

Such men, and such only, are really calculated to do lasting good among Indians; men who are not afraid to blacken their hands by logging the timber; men who are not ashamed to work in their shirt sleeves; men who do not say to the Indians, "Go and do this or that," but who say to them, "Come on, brethren": such men only can convince the Indians that they are their friends and wish to do them good . . . The Indian is a free man and will not be driven. Gain his confidence and esteem, and then you can do anything with him.

– Quoted in *Sacred Feathers*, pp. 81, 82

XXIII The Ottawa Connection

On December 16th, 1959, he was called to Ottawa to meet Indian Affairs Branch officials to discuss the situation in Indian schools. This led to a major assignment: preparing a brief for the government on behalf of the United Church. He was assisted by a small committee, but writing—and presenting—the brief was his responsibility.

It was called a brief, but that's a misnomer. It is lengthy and comprehensive. There is room here for only an outline, but I would like to quote one paragraph that urged the government to regard the church as its ally in implementing plans for development:

> We believe that the United Church of Canada, by its traditions, its form of government, and its emphasis on lay participation is particularly fitted to encourage and train the people for self-government and increased responsibility in their own community and in the nation. An important feature of our work among the Indians has been the leadership and activity of its Indian members, which have frequently persisted in spite of our inability to provide sufficient missionaries. The Church has done more than any other agency to prepare Indian men and women for positions of responsibility at the local level. It is therefore in a good position to emphasize this aspect of administration in the future. We earnestly suggest that government agencies should not overlook the Church as an effective partner in any programs aimed at encouraging participation by the Indian people.

One section on the Indian Act is particularly hard-hitting in its demand for specific changes. And yet, Elgie laconically reported: "The Brief was well received." Indeed, Sen. Gladstone, the first and only Indian senator, said that the brief raised every issue that should be raised. Here is a summary of the report:

OUTLINE

INTRODUCTION: Main points of emphasis.

1. *Co-operation, between both government and voluntary agencies at all levels.*

2. *Responsibility of Indians in their own affairs; encouragement and opportunity.*

THE CONTRIBUTION OF THE CHURCH

1. *The importance of religion in a society.*
2. *The Church leads men to Jesus Christ:*
   The dignity and worth of every individual,
   The power to achieve the best.
3. *The United Church encourages local leadership and trains for responsibility.*
4. *The Church provides trained leaders for Indian communities.*

CO-OPERATION

1. *Economic Development.*
2. *Social and Cultural Development.*
3. *Education.*
4. *Health Services.*
5. *Administration.*

RESPONSIBILITY

1. *Indians should be encouraged to share in all areas of collaborative work.*
2. *Indians will assume responsibility if given the opportunity.*

THE INDIAN ACT

1. *The Indians should be given the Federal vote, without loss of rights and privileges.*

2. *There should be a Department of Indian Affairs with its own Minister and Deputy Minister.*
3. *Indians should have the right of appeal against decisions of the Minister.*
4. *Provision should be made for more credit for responsible Indians and groups of Indians.*
5. *There should be clarification of the Section on Trespassing.*
6. *There should be a continuing Research Committee on Indian Affairs.*

CONCLUSION

This brief explains the issues in broad general terms;
The need for flexibility in applying principles.

There is a current series on CBC-TV called *On the Road Again*. That might well be the title of this story. Perhaps Elgie enjoyed this part of his job more than the office work and interminable meetings at H.Q. There is a whole binder called “Field Trips” giving full accounts of his journeys. They must have required a lot of stamina; and there were many meetings on these trips also where difficult decisions must often have been made.

A 1960 trip to B.C. had plenty of variety in its programme. At Hazelton there was an all-day presbytery meeting dealing with Indian problems in the many matters where they had responsibility. There was a visit to Kispiox, a salmon-fishing village, to discuss the school situation, and then one to Kilzegucla for an evening service where the Indians were eager to show off their new electric organ. A little portable generator powered both organ and lights, and whenever the music called for full organ, the light almost went out. No such problems had been encountered with the old pedal/reed organ.

Then it was on to Prince Rupert to discuss a new Friendship House. Problems were already emerging as Indians drifted to towns and cities from the reserves where there was little employment. Drop-in centres and hostels were badly needed. From there Elgie went to Vancouver to catch the ferry to Nanaimo in order to assess the Alberni Residential School.

The scandal that erupted in the late nineties involving charges against a lay assistant for sexual involvement with several of the boys was then far in the future. The school was highly regarded in the community and provided educational opportunity to pupils from isolated areas in B.C. It was the largest of the United Church schools, with 292 in residence, of whom 140 in Grades VII to XII attended the local high school. There was a resident Christian Education director, and sixteen senior students taught Sunday school classes. This institution stood high in the opinion of the Indian Affairs branch.

Knowing Elgie's reservations about such institutions, it is interesting to see his report to the Home Missions Board after a visit:

> Despite a good deal of misunderstanding, our residential schools are making a very important contribution to the lives of the young people attending them. *While they cannot hope to duplicate the better features of life in home and family*, the educational facilities at least are much superior to those otherwise available to them . . .

In his report on residential schools in general, he noted (with some satisfaction) that their role was gradually changing. In areas where more integration was possible and desirable (the situation Chief Peter Jones faced in southwest Ontario a century before), they were becoming more and more like hostels for students from inadequately-schooled areas and sending them to neighbouring public and high schools. The exception was Norway House, which served a vast, sparsely settled area. And no longer were Indian agents almost forcing parents to send their children "out." There was a large waiting list for the schools. Elgie was recommending that those who had had the "advantage" of two or three years inside be given accommodations with suitable families so others could share the advantage that parents now believed valuable.

His last stop was back at Vancouver for a very interesting event that showed the church taking advantage of modern technology. He was invited to dedicate the first of the church's mission planes, the "George Pringle," a Cessna-180 to be operated out of Alert Bay. The missionary/pilot could now reach distant outports in a fraction of the time the mission boat took, and if needed, could take a patient to the hospital in a hurry. This had already proven to be the case at God's Lake Narrows, Manitoba, where the Rev. George Millard flew his own plane.

Meetings awaited Elgie at home. A while before, the Indian-Eskimo (note the *two* now passé terms) Association had been formed, and he was not only on the executive, but was chair of the membership committee. Three days of his first week back were devoted to planning the association's first annual meeting, which took up another two days in Ottawa. He had a week at his desk, and then he was off again in response to a call from the superintendent of Home Missions in Saskatchewan. In Muncey he had helped prevent the closing of Mt. Elgin Residential School until a better replacement was ready. The two residential schools in Saskatchewan had been closed without such preparation, and the best had to be made of a bad situation. Then, to take advantage of this visit, along with the Rev. Armand Stade, he toured all the reserves in southern Saskatchewan, piling up a mileage of 1,025 (miles, not yet kilometers).

He was not through in the West yet. A situation had arisen in the school at Edmonton where his old friend from the Muncey Institute days, Rev. O. B. Strapp, was the principal, that needed immediate attention: an illicit relationship between two employees. Mr. Strapp felt it keenly because he was a longtime friend of one of those involved. Resolving this required the resignation of one of the two, but a court case was threatened. Since Mr. Strapp was due to retire in June, Elgie suggested that he do so instead at Christmas so that he would not be further drained by staying on. This he did, and joined Mrs. Strapp who was "Down East" for medical attention. After appointing an acting principal, Elgie returned to Toronto for more meetings, some, like a Rural Life Conference at Horning's Mills, involving keynote addresses.

Ottawa seemed to be on his agenda more frequently. In January of '61 he was there again, this time for a meeting of the Education Subcommittee of the Indian Affairs Department. He was able to fraternize at these meetings with his fellow-appointees from other denominations. This time he "went to bat" for the children of Sandy Lake where he had recently dedicated the new church. The government was about to build a new school there. Its regional superintendent wanted it built near the store and nursing station. That meant that the children would have to cross the lake, in summer by boat; in winter, across the ice. Elgie was persuasive; the superintendent would have to cross the lake.

XXIV "But the Labourers Are Few"

After four years of intensive work, and with a thorough knowledge of how things were going, he was able to give an optimistic report to the board. In 1957 he had found a good deal of disillusionment among the workers, and an apparent retreat all along the line. He believed now that the tide had turned, and that if they took advantage of it, it would "lead on to fortune." He gave credit to the better quality of workers, to more enthusiastic participation by the Indians themselves and to a different attitude in the presbyteries, for example, their initiative in the Sandy Lake area. He had been particularly impressed by the devotion of many Indian lay-leaders and local preachers. He valued the work of training sessions that brought whites and Indians together and overcame their sense of isolation. As examples he pointed to the annual conference at Five Oaks near Paris, Ontario, initiated by himself and Dr. Stokes, the area superintendent, while Elgie had still been at Muncey; and the recent annual Bible School at Norway House. He assisted at both every year. In fact, he gave credit to everyone—but himself.

Yet he was not blind to a major weakness in the system: the rapid turnover of workers. He brought attention to this gently but unmistakably in one of his regular letters, "To Those Who Represent the United Church Among the Indian People." This one on June 22nd, 1962, is ostensibly (and no doubt genuinely) to thank "those who are leaving our work, in gratitude for their devotion and efforts on behalf of our people." He lists the names of the fourteen, their areas of service, and the length of that service. He does not need to point out that the average was only three years.

He puts a good face on this. They will now help in "building up a company of friends of the Indian work throughout the Church, and they can make an important contribution in recruiting and in promoting better attitudes toward Indian people." Then he notes that the ones who are best at this are those who have stayed on the job at least five years. A plea to those who were not leaving? At least they knew he had stayed twenty years before serving in his present capacity.

In the same letter he pays tribute to the remarkable loyalty of Mr.

F. J. Dodson: fifty years as a missionary teacher. He had worked with Grandfather Joblin in Red Deer, Alberta; he had been a senior teacher at Muncey, giving Elgie fine support through those years; he had been at Moraviantown and then at Saugeen, returning on retirement to Moraviantown to set up the Indian Museum there. Early in his work at the board, Elgie had set up a retirement plan for lay workers. No one ever deserved it more than Mr. Dodson.

He was the exception. Elgie's lament for the scarcity of trained, long-term workers comes out strongly in his report on Newfoundland. He was not there on behalf of his beloved Indians, but as a member of the Board of Home Missions. On the retirement of John Leng from the board, his work was allocated to the others, including a new member, George Morrison. George had been a top man in IBM; with his outstanding ability he was soon recruited from the pastorate, following his ordination, to this administrative work, then to be treasurer of the United Church, and finally to be secretary of the General Council. After his retirement from *that* he was called to Timothy Eaton Memorial Church. Elgie asked for the portfolio of Maritime missions. He was well acquainted with its work on the west coast, and he wanted to know the East as well. So from September 25th to October 16th of 1961 he made a thorough tour of Newfoundland.

He came to love the people there. Perhaps that was partly because they had retained much of the old Methodist way that he remembered fondly from his youth. But he was appalled at the shortage of trained workers in the church, and the overwork of those who were there. In the smallest presbytery, Twillingate (where he preached on Sunday and was impressed by the choir), there were seven lay supplies, most of them inexperienced. The ministerial members had to serve on several committees. On the drive across the island with Dr. Butt, the superintendent of missions, he saw the devastation wrought by a widespread forest fire that robbed many of employment. People were moving out. The coastal fisheries had not yet been hit by the cod shortage, but emigration from inland had already begun to affect Newfoundland. At Carmanville, for instance, eleven houses had been destroyed, and the fire had burned to within forty feet of the church. Some were asking why they had been burned out even though they were church supporters. Elgie commented, "a challenge to the ministers."

Everywhere he went (and it seemed to be everywhere) he preached in the church and visited a school. This was long before Premier Brian Tobin had managed to change the long-standing situation in which every denomination had the right to its own school. Elgie soon found the reasons why the United Church wanted this changed. They were already cooperating with the Anglicans where new schools were needed. In one community, for instance, Anglicans had helped the United Church build a two-room school on the south side, and vice versa on the north. Now the Pentecostals planned to build one. The Salvation Army already had one. In each case, the minister was usually chairman of the board of education. If he had three appointments, this added to his burden. And of course the quality of education suffered with so many all-grade one-room schools where there should have been several rooms, able to teach different grades including high school.

The removal of whole villages from picturesque "outports," so dear to Joey Smallwood's heart, was by no means complete. The failure of the cod fisheries would accomplish that. Even the larger ports with fish-packing plants, to which many had moved, would suffer in the future. There were few roads to these outports, so boats were the means of transportation. I was surprised to find so many as-yet-populated islands. The first he visited was Change Islands. There was a U. C. mission boat for this area, the *Messenger*, but it was out of commission, so Dr. Butt hired one. The communion service was the first in three years; lay supplies were not permitted to lead these, perform weddings or baptisms. From there they went to Fogo Island, but were delayed a day by a storm at sea. The lay supply there was Cecil Eveleigh, who had been at it for eighteen years—surely he deserved a Doctor of Divinity (honoris causa). After a baptismal service there, they went on to Joe Batt's Arm (no explanation of the name) to dedicate a new church hall, and visited Seldom-Come-By and Stag Harbour. Elgie was impressed by how well all the churches were cared for, their white paint glistening in the sun.

Then again they went by boat to New World Island. It must be a big one, judging by the churches visited: Herring Neck, Merritt's Harbour, Virgin Arm, Tissett's Harbour, Moreton Harbour, Bridgeport, Carter's Cove, Comfort Cove.

Back on the mainland, he spoke at the Grand Falls presbytery meeting in Botwood and then saw the devastation caused by a recent fire at the dock. A warehouse with 5,000 tons of paper burned, as did a ship with another 3,000 tons. How many trees did that represent? The next day he spoke at the assembly of the United Church High School to 192 pupils. He left no record of his subject.

Then they went by boat again from Little Burnt Arm to Exploits, where he preached to a small congregation. A year earlier there had been twenty-four U. C. families; now there were twelve, and the pessimists thought it would be empty in another year. As it was, the minister from Little Burnt Arm could get there only every six weeks. The people got a radio broadcast of a U. C. service. Elgie suggested that they meet in homes for this, with a discussion afterward.

The trip to Cottrell's Cove took two and one-half hours over very stormy seas. Dr. Butt was an experienced pilot and seemed to enjoy the challenge. The village was spread all round the cove, which Elgie found beautiful. As usual, Elgie preached on Sunday. There were U.C. and Salvation Army schools. Recently the Pentecostals had moved in, built a hall, and planned another school. Everywhere they seemed to have ample funds. Some said it came from their H.Q. in the United States. They themselves said it came from tithing.

Finally, before being taken to Gander airport and St. John's, there was a boat trip (on the *Sailor's Dream*) to Point Leamington. He preached and conducted communion there while Dr. Butt went on to Paradise to do the same. After all this time with the superintendent, Elgie was quite sure that he belonged in Paradise. The people of Newfoundland would heartily agree.

On the way home there were stopovers, first at Halifax to confer with immigration officials, then for a longer stay in Montreal. He visited the Pointe Aux Trembles School, preached at Oka and Caughnawaga, took the night train to Toronto, arrived at 8:00 a.m., and was in his office at 9:30. There was a Methodist hymn that urged us to "Give every flying minute something to keep in store."

XXV Marble Halls and Indian Floors

Elgie never dreamt of marble halls, but he must have felt that he had entered into an approximation of them when, sometime before, "Church House" was moved from its old quarters at 299 Queen Street West to the new ones at 89 St. Clair Avenue East. These were more adequate to a church that had grown since 1915 when the old Methodist Book Room had been built. The building was light and airy, had good committee rooms, and a lovely chapel where the occupants took turns leading daily prayers. Then in May of '62 he and Helen bought their first home, close to the new H.Q. (affectionately called the "Vatican") at 109 Inglewood Drive, with a small down payment and a large mortgage. You might say that he thus joined the silent majority of middle-class Canadians.

Just at that time his faithful old car passed away. So he bought his first new one—a little French Simca imported by Chrysler to join their "stable" at the bottom end. He was fond of that car. It did not return his affection. One day when he was backing out of the narrow garage the engine stalled and burst into flame. To add to the misfortune, it stalled just when his doors were beside the garage door frame. He was trapped. Fortunately the Simca had a standard transmission. Leaving it in reverse he held the starter down until the car slowly backed and he could leap out. John Wesley, the founder of Methodism, told of the time his father's rectory burned. The little lad made it to a window and was rescued by a neighbour just as the burning thatch fell in. He called himself "a brand plucked from the burning." In Elgie's case a good battery took the place of the neighbour.

As for Indian floors—on which he had slept previously—they were on his mind in his mid-winter tour of Manitoba missions. After three months of desk work, innumerable meetings including two in Ottawa with the Department of Indian Affairs, he set out for a five-week visit to this province with so many struggling mission stations. The meetings in Winnipeg, where one concern was the number of Indians who had drifted in from reserves, and in the residential schools, would not be too bad even at 30 below. The far North was different. He spent three days with the Terry Whytes at Sandy Lake before going to Sioux

Lookout for the presbytery. Two of these days were spent trying to get a heavy hose and pump to the lake through deep snow. Their cistern was empty and Terry did not want to leave his wife without water. Terry was young. Elgie could have used a convenient floor to rest on occasionally.

And ditto for Island Lake. After services there with Rev. George Millard in the morning and afternoon, they trudged through the snow for several miles for an evening service in a home. In the dark he kept stumbling off the path into snow banks. It was a real test of his stamina.

Mr. Millard was the supervisor for the work at Red Sucker Lake, which was served by an Indian lay supply, Adam Fiddler. They had two interesting days with the Fiddlers and their flock and experienced real Indian hospitality. Their house had only one room and a lean-to. Their hosts insisted that the two guests take the bed, while they slept on the floor in the lean-to. During the day everybody gathered in the church to talk about problems and discuss the booklet *Life and Death*. When mealtime came, the women went home and brought whatever they had—pots of rabbit or moose stew and bannocks. A sheet of plastic was spread on the floor and everyone sat on the floor too. They tossed the bones on the plastic; when all was eaten, they shook the plastic outside for the dogs. The next morning as they were eating breakfast two friends came in. Mrs. Fiddler served them, then took her plate and sat on the floor—no room at the table.

Incidentally, an illustration of the Indians' spirit of sharing seen in the coastal custom of "potlatch," was evident in a small way the previous day. Two children had birthdays, and two cakes had been brought. There were not enough pieces for everyone. The children had none! But they seemed happy—honoured—that their cakes had been shared. They had probably never heard that "It is more blessed to give than to receive." This truth was simply part of their culture. Elgie took note of it because it was the essence of his own character. Again and again at the end of one of these "duty" tours, he would remark, "Tired, but happy that something seemed to have been achieved." "Exhausted physically, but spiritually refreshed."

XXVI Two Press Tempests

(See Appendix V)

In 1960 the papers in Ontario carried horror stories about starvation around Nelson House, Manitoba. To ascertain the facts, Elgie made "a very strenuous tour of northern Manitoba." After visiting all the reserves and talking to Indian leaders he concluded that the reports had been greatly exaggerated. Their standards of living were low by Ontario city standards, but there was no starvation. On the way out he stopped at The Pas to visit a sanitarium run by old friends, Dr. Hayward and his wife Ruth, who had been his classmate through five years of high school in Stirling. He found the people in The Pas indignant over the bad press the North had received, and he was asked to speak about the situation Sunday at the church. No one told him in advance that it was broadcast, but he said he heard no negative reactions.

There was a much bigger furore two years later. This time the Toronto press went beyond charges of starvation. They blamed INCO, in Thompson, Manitoba, for unemployment on account of their refusal to hire Indian workers. Again Elgie was asked to investigate. The list of places visited sounds like an announcement in Union Station of an imminent departure. "Winnipeg, Fisher River, Lynn Lake, South Indian Lake, Nelson House, Oxford House, Thompson, Norway House, Cross Lake, and The Pas." This time he wrote a full report, which was published as "Our Northern Indians." It is a careful analysis of the problems facing both Indians and employers, and urges the right of Indians to choose their way of life. They could decide between punching time clocks with the resultant ability to purchase the luxuries whites regard as necessities, or the traditional way of hunting and trapping with occasional periods of hardship stoically endured. This report shows such understanding of the First Nations that it is included in Appendix V. Perhaps Peter Newman had learned something from our aborigines when he gave as his "Fifth Commandment" to university graduates, "Reject the assumption that more is necessarily better; that efficiency and material gain are the ultimate goal of human activity. They are not" (*Maclean's*, June 21st, 1999).

XXVII A Little Home Life, Please

With such an agenda: field trips spring, fall and winter, meetings with presbyteries in Ontario, participating annually in the Five Oaks study-conferences for Indian workers, and committee meetings too numerous to mention, was he ever at home? Well, those committee meetings were usually in Toronto; on the frequent Ottawa trips for the department, the Indian-Eskimo Association, and now interdenominational meetings, he would take a night train home and be there for breakfast. On Sundays when he was not speaking somewhere, he and Helen would be at Metropolitan Church together.

Occasionally they would spend an evening with us in North York where he could indulge his old passion for homemade music: two accordions, a clarinet, and a melodica. The two women could ignore us while they chatted. Summer holidays? He stayed home, with occasional visits to Helen's sister Esther and brother-in-law Ray Williams in Campbellford and to Dad in Port Perry. In that summer, when Dad was obviously failing, they got out to see him most weekends. He died in his ninety-first year, and all the family was there for the funeral. Probably next to Gladys who had cared for him so long, no one missed him more than Elgie, for whom his father had been both inspiration and pattern. But think of the satisfaction Dad had received from Elgie's career! The seed had brought forth 100-fold.

His January 1964 tour of B.C. missions included some interesting experiences. At Campbell River, the Marine Planning Committee met on the aging *Thomas Crosby IV*, partly to discuss how long the old craft would be serviceable and whether the board would pay for a new one, specifically designed for its tasks. Elgie advised them to obtain specifications and costs. This was done; the boat was eventually built—with a large cost overrun. Thirty years later the B.C. government would have the same experience with a new super ferry.

There was a "first" at Cape Mudge. Elgie and the area superintendent, Oliver Howard, urged the Indians to issue a "call" to William Robinson of Klemtu, and helped them with the form for the presbytery. This was the first call by an Indian congregation to an Indian minister. All went well.

Arriving the next day at Alert Bay, Elgie had the opportunity of meeting the second of the pilot/missionaries for the "George Pringle" plane, Bob Burrows (who happened to be one of my former favourite pupils at Victoria College).[1] Then Bob took off with his father-in-law, Dr. Frank Fiddler, to go to Port McNeill and prepare for the next day's special service. It was indeed special. The new church was shared by the Anglicans. Archdeacon Ellis of Columbia Mission and Elgie presided at the dedication, Dr. Fiddler preached, and Bob Burrows conducted. The people would long remember this. Their memory would be aided by the failure of the lights during supper, the result of a heavy snowfall.

On Monday he was picked up by the Crosby for the long trip to Bella Coola, the H.Q. hospital for Dr. Donald Watt, who was on board. An unforgettable journey followed. They bucked a strong nor'easter for over twelve hours. For five of them Elgie stood, braced out of the way behind the wheelsman, to enjoy the show—and caught a cold. Because the rigging was icing up so badly that they might capsize, they anchored for the night in a sheltered cove. Twice the next day they tried again, only to be forced to turn around and head for Namu. Taking advantage of the opportunity, Elgie inspected a new fish plant and Dr. Watt operated on a man's foot. That evening they caught the steamer *Northland Prince*, reached Bella Coola near midnight, and then went on to Prince Rupert. According to Elgie's brief notes, the next five days went like this:

Jan. 25 *Saturday. In Prince Rupert.*
Visited Miss Sharpe and Friendship House. Late lunch with Dr. Watt.
2:00 for afternoon and evening. Again stayed in to check cold, in order to make trip on Sunday to Port Simpson.

Jan. 26 *Sunday.*
11:30 picked up by Dr. Watt, taken to Seal Cove to catch plane to Port Simpson.
Cessna 180, 15 minutes (3 hours by boat).
Lunch at the school with Miss Daly and other teachers. Mrs.

[1] In 2001, Bob was awarded a D.D. degree by his alma mater.

Cashore being away.
Afternoon with John Cashore; saw some of the village.
Dinner at the school.
Service at the church, 7:00 to 8:30. Good choir.
Afterward at the manse, social gathering with singing and refreshments, until 11:00 p.m. Good fellowship.

Jan. 27 Monday.
Breakfast at manse.
Visited all 7 classrooms of the school.
Toured the village, meeting a number of people. Some good pictures.
12:30 to 12:45 Trip back to Prince Rupert.
2:00 - 3:30 with Jack Murdoch and Dr. Watt.
Back to hotel. 5:40 picked up by Bob Elliott, who took me home to dinner.
7:30 went to Friendship House for meeting of the Board; followed by coffee with chairman, Mr. Forward, Mr. Barnes (I.A.), Murdoch, Watt.

Jan. 28 Tuesday.
8:15 picked up by Dr. Watt for trip to Sandspit and Skidegate—bus and ferry to airport, DC 6 to Sandspit, weather rough; bus and boat to Skidegate, arriving at noon. I had lunch with Bells (deer meat and octopus), Dr. Watt going to Dr. Archibald's.
Afternoon with Mr. Bell. Visited hospital, Miss Wellington, Queen Charlotte church.
6:00 Supper at the hall prepared by U.C.W. of Skidegate.
8:00 Congregational meeting (Skidegate).
10:30 to 12:15 discussion with Mr. and Mrs. Bell.

Jan. 29 Wednesday.
7:15 left for boat and bus to Sandspit. Had breakfast there with Watt and Bell.
Dr. Watt took plane to Prince Rupert. I stayed for 1 1/2 hour visit with Mr. Bell.

When plane returned from Prince Rupert, it reported damage to wing flap.
Settled down to wait for another plane to be rerouted from Smithers.
It came—at 6:15 p.m.!
6:15 boarded plane for Vancouver, reaching there about 9:30 p.m.
Met there by Mr. Sieber. Visited for an hour before catching TCA for Toronto.

Jan. 30 Thursday.
Reached home 8:45 a.m. Time to clean up, have breakfast and get to office by 9:20 and the meeting of the Executive.

XXVIII Two Experiences of Sharing

In the spring of that year, under the auspices of the Canadian Council of Churches, the first meeting of "The Inter-Church Consultation on Indian Work" was held in Ottawa. Elgie represented the United Church and gave a paper on the extent and aims of its work. (This is included in "Field Trips," as are the texts of all his addresses.) One of his concerns was the confusing effect on the Indians of competing denominations and an appeal to tackle the problem. In his section on education, he probably raised some hackles by saying:

> We believe that the education of Indian youth is the responsibility of the Federal Government and that we should move toward the time when the Churches will have no more control here than they have for other Canadian youth . . . Hence we co-operate with the Government in their emphasis on "integrated" schools, and their movement away from large institutional residences to day-schools and private boarding homes.

This was "a history-making meeting" not only in interdenominational terms, but because there were three speakers representing the Indians, one from Ontario, one from Manitoba, and one from Alberta. Elgie must have been happy at this indication that his goal of working with, not just for, the Indians was being implemented.

The other experience demanded much more preparation, and he spent much of the summer working on it. Every year the ministers in Northern Ontario met for a conference they called the Lorrain Fellowship. It offered them a time of study, inspiration, and sharing of problems, since they served in more isolation than those in the south. For the conference in September 1964, they asked Elgie to give three keynote lectures on the Indians of Canada. He was more than pleased; these delegates lived close to much of the aboriginal population of Ontario and could help implement the plans of the Home Mission Board. In his introduction he said:

> I must try to avoid reacting to this opportunity in the manner described by Mr. Percy Bird, one of the outstanding Indians in Manitoba, when he was asked to speak at our Conference of Indian workers in Winnipeg. He began by saying, "A chance to address so many church workers makes me feel like a mosquito in a nudist colony." I feel more like a person who has come to a Sunday School picnic, where each family brings its own generous contribution to the meal.

He then proposed to divide the three talks as follows: the Indian situation as it is today; a history of past interactions; and hopes and plans for the future. "In other words, 'Where Are We?', 'How Did We Get Here?' and 'Where Are We Going?'"

These addresses showed such a grasp of the whole picture that they deserved wider circulation than to this small group. It is remarkable that most of the insights still apply, though the talks were given thirty-five years ago. The biggest changes are the rapidity of change today (though along the lines Elgie suggested) and the sharpness of the current criticisms of church and government. One would expect that as a churchman he would deal primarily with moral and spiritual issues, but he gave equal attention to the economic and social concerns. He did not compartmentalize life, but treated the relationships among all aspects as parts of an integrated whole. And he was concerned with Metis and the urbanized as well as reserve Indians. He dwells on the continuing discrimination, no doubt because his listeners were in a position to do something about it. (I could wish that he had recommended a reading of Fred Bodsworth's novel *The Strange One*, dealing as it does with their own area of Ontario.)

After discussing the diversity of customs in the many "Nations" from coast to coast, he deals with a question now much to the fore, "aboriginal spirituality." I quote him quoting himself from his pamphlet *Out of the Tepee* published by the Indian-Eskimo Association:

> The religious beliefs and practices of the Indians varied widely also, so that one hesitates to make any general statements about them. Much that has been too hastily

labeled "superstition" was the expression of a deeply religious nature. The Indians were keenly aware of the influences of the forces of nature upon their lives and of their dependence upon them. They sought to please and appease these forces, to gain their favour and help. It seemed reasonable to suppose that spirits animated all animals and nature even as mankind was, and should be treated with proper respect. Especially was this true of those animals on which they depended most for their very lives. Elaborate rules grew up for the proper treatment of those animals so that their "spirits" would not be offended and withdraw, leaving the Indians to starve. Each group had its unwritten code that was enforced by public opinion, and since the individual could not survive apart from the group, their rules of conduct were really effective.

> It was their highest ambition to establish contact with the supernatural, to obtain some mark of favour and the guidance and help of some spirit for their lives. Thus it was a quite general practice to seek an "experience" in which some guardian spirit appeared and accepted responsibility for the person, a very individual matter that played a vital part throughout the person's whole life. By isolating themselves, by fasting, by prayer, and sometimes by the purifying effects of the sweat lodge, they sought, and usually found, a guardian spirit.

In order to understand what may irritate "whites" about Indians, he quotes from a Dakota Sioux the concepts of our culture that are foreign to most of them:

> 1. Sustained work, on a regular time-table. Among Indians there was a clear division of labour between men and women. Men knew what it was to work hard when it was required, and developed great powers of endurance.

2. Saving for the future—usually impossible anyway. One of the more difficult habits for Indians to acquire is to deny oneself a present good for the sake of a greater good in the future.

3. Time, as we think of it. It is not measured by minutes but by "moons." There is no word for "being late."

4. Different attitudes to sharing—with them it was ingrained because essential for the survival of the tribe.

To these Elgie adds a characteristic that has developed because of the well-meant but short-sighted habit of governments and churches—the results of paternalism. We have made them too dependent on us, too unsure of themselves. Decisions have been made for them. In this, Elgie practiced what he preached. As an illustration of this, when he was involved in the "starvation" furore that we mentioned earlier, a charity organization in England sent over funds that were spent on generous food hampers for each family. Elgie urged them to look upon this as a Christmas gift, and not to become dependent on constant "handouts."

To balance the list above, Elgie lists *our* tendencies that irritate Indians. We are too aggressive; too talkative, uneasy at silence; too domineering; too zealous (especially for our own denomination); too self-righteous; too fond of physical comfort; too enslaved by time; too concerned with knowing and not concerned enough about being; too obsessed by "success" in comparison with others. It would be salutary for us, to quote Burns, to see ourselves as others see us.

It was stated earlier that Indians should be allowed to choose whether to continue in their old culture (where this was still possible, i.e., on the reserves, especially in the North) or adjust to the dominant one around them. But Elgie pointed out that the former option was less and less viable, if for no other reason than the dwindling stocks of fur-bearing animals, the poor return on them, and the lessening demand. The growing demand for self-government and the needs for self-sustaining industries to give employment also pointed to needs for better educational opportunities and technical training.

But, he continued, would it not be possible for them to make these adjustments and still retain valuable elements from their historic culture? And if they learn from us—and experience has shown that where learning has been slow it has not been because of a disparity in intelligence but because of faulty education—is it not possible for us to learn from them? Perhaps our arrogance makes this the more unlikely of the two! Of immediate importance is the removal of prejudice and misunderstanding on both sides so that we can live well together as fellow Canadians.

That these lectures were appreciated is shown by a warm letter of commendation from Norman Vale of the *United Church Observer*. He thought that they could be used as background material for writers of a series of stories incorporating their many insights.

XXIX A Different Kind of Conference

From early in his Muncey days Elgie had been sent as a delegate to the triennial National Fellowship of Indian Workers that met in Estes Park, Colorado. Although he gave an occasional paper, was listed as a resource leader after his appointment to the Board of Home Missions, and was elected First Vice-President in 1964, his journal shows that he was on the receiving end most of the time. Looking back on those years when he was given so much information and inspiration, and where he made so many friends both white and Indian, he wrote:

> It is doubtful whether anyone will ever attempt to evaluate the impact of the Fellowship on our work in Canada through those of us who were privileged to attend. For myself, I am convinced that it did much to broaden our horizons and make us more aware of the basic unity that existed among us. For the most part we Canadians are a silent people, slow to express appreciation or gratitude, much less any genuine love for others who may have meant a great deal to us . . . There were quite a few Indian men and women whom I came to know as genuine friends and whom I anticipated meeting every three years with deep joy. Altogether it was an enriching experience for which I shall always be grateful.

XXX An Ideal Indian Missionary

In Canada's Centennial Year the Indians of Northern Alberta celebrated by dedicating a new church at Goodfish Lake to the memory of an Ojibwa from Ontario. This remarkable man could stand as Elgie's ideal—an aboriginal with the advantages of education who mediated the Christian message through his own culture. In his journal he included a copy of *Northern Lights* for September 1967 that gives the story, under the title "Highlights from the Oldest Mission in Northern Alberta, Goodfish-Whitefish Lakes and Saddle Lake Larger Parish, in the United Church of Canada."

In 1820 a boy was born on the shores of Lake Couchiching, Ontario, whose name was Big Sail. As a lad he was adopted by a man who had just lost his son, and took his name, Henry Bird Steinhauer. He was trained as a teacher, agriculturalist, and minister. He helped James Evans translate the Bible into the Cree syllabic, as well as many gospel songs. In 1855 he went to the Whitefish area of Alberta and was a formative influence in every way, since Plains Cree was closely related to his native tongue. Here is the tribute to him from the Indians of Goodfish Lake:

> He was first of all the Messenger of the Great Spirit.
> He was a prophet, preacher, teacher, agriculturalist.
>
> He came as one of us,
> He dwelt among us,
> He understood us,
> He spoke our language,
> He taught the Scriptures in our language.
>
> He helped us educationally,
> He helped us economically,
> He helped us personally.
> He was aware of our culture.
> He was a man who knew agriculture.
> He was well-versed in Holy Scripture.

> We shall always remember him because he brought a message of everlasting hope to our people.

His contribution to Alberta continued through his family. His two sons were ordained ministers. The younger became Lt. Governor of Alberta. I was privileged to be present when Victoria University gave a D.D. degree to Robert Bird Steinhauer in April 1937. He had been the first Indian with a B.A. to be ordained. He graduated from Victoria College in 1887 when it was still in Cobourg, and though he was the only Indian there he was so popular he earned the Senior Stick. When he was presented for the doctorate fifty years later, Dr. Jesse Arnup said, "We honour him for historic reasons and for his own worth as a man, as a Christian missionary, and as a minister of the United Church of Canada."

In the same Centennial issue of *Northern Lights*, the Indian editor, Chief John Snow, commented on "the quiet revolution" that was changing his people. This transformation affected life on the reserves as well as among those whose training and initiative showed that they could make a contribution to Canadian life outside the reserves. As Snow observes:

> Our Church has a great opportunity and has a very important role to play in helping Indians help themselves within this quiet revolution. It will continue until every Indian receives equality, justice, freedom, and the numerous opportunities that every other Canadian has.

XXXI The Indians of Canada

In 1967, Elgie also produced a large pamphlet that was printed and sent to all the churches in Canada to foster better understanding of their fellow citizens. In an introduction Dr. M. C. Macdonald wrote:

> The Canadian Indian is today very much in the news. However, as Rev. E. E. M. Joblin implies in his article, too many who purport to write and speak for the Indians are non-Indian. He reasons that instead of trying to speak for the Indians, we should make it possible for capable and informed Indian leaders to speak for themselves. Mr. Joblin had had many years of experience in working with the Indian people—for 21 years as missionary and then as educator, and latterly as an administrator of his Church's program of service to its Indian constituency. He can speak with authority.

The pamphlet is well illustrated with pictures of Indians engaged in many activities, and is full of all kinds of information. An example is the listing of "The Extent of the Work Today":

> 76 congregations
> 3 church-owned student residences
> 4 government-financed, church-run residences
> 2 reception lodges (Vancouver, Winnipeg)
> 1 halfway house for girls
> 3 full-time urban workers
> 1 community worker
> 7 hospitals
> 1 mission boat, 1 aircraft

The list goes on, and notes grants to eight organizations such as Friendship Centres.

One bit of information must have given him particular pleasure to write:

> The long uphill battle to get the Indian children into school has been largely won. In 1945 there were 16,000 enrolled in schools. Today there are 62,000. At this time 95% of all Indian children of school age are in school. Where a nominal 100 were attending High School in 1945 today there are more than 5,000. Where we had no record of Indians taking post-High School training then, today we have over 5,000 taking University, Technical, and other adult-education courses.

The pamphlet ends with some quotations from Indians. Ruth Muskrat Bronson has written:

> The government schools are teaching youth how to make a living, but it is the Church that must tell them how to live courageously and wisely, motivated and directed by spiritual power.
>
> Indian youth, like other youth, cannot find within themselves the strength or the vision to solve the intolerable difficulties that confront them. Only religion can provide the ideals and guide to right living urgently needed to help them achieve a more abundant life economically, socially, and spiritually, and to lead the white world into a more general acceptance of individuals.

On the last point, Chief Summers, a Muncey Ontario schoolteacher, at the Ontario Federation of Home and School Associations, suggested that the quickest way to the acceptance of Indians by non-Indians was their integration into regular schools.

And finally there is this request from the Indian Pavilion at Expo '67: "Give us the right to manage our own affairs!"

XXXII 1968-69: More of the Usual—with an Exception

We are familiar by now with Elgie's full calendar of activities: four "tours" a year; at home, weeks full of meetings and correspondence, often with preaching on Sundays. The only one of these trips I will mention is described in a diary entry dated February 9th, 1967. It involved successive nights of wearying train travel. After listing the meetings, the diary says:

> Evening train for Noranda, a long night trip through Northern Ontario into Quebec. Spent Sunday there, speaking at Church, meeting Board, and several families who were boarding Indian students. Not sure I was much help, but perhaps some encouragement and the appreciation of the Church for what they were trying to do. Back to Toronto on the night train.

And now let us speak of something exceptional. For many years Elgie had been a member of a committee sponsored by Indian Affairs in Ottawa. This was in a department whose names, and ministers, had changed over the years. Now it was the Department of Indian Affairs and Northern Development, and the minister a young Jean Chrétien.

This committee dealt with many routine matters, such as the relation of the government and the churches in their long partnership in education. Elgie had reiterated his concern for a greater participation of the aborigines themselves. There were none in the department, though there was now one senator, Mr. Gladstone. At last the Honourable Jean Chrétien announced a new proposal in Parliament on June 25th, 1969. I quote its introduction, as set forth in a special issue of *The Indian News*:

New Policy For Indians

The Government believes that its policies must lead to the full, free and non-discriminatory participation of the Indian people in Canadian society. Such a goal requires a break with the past. It requires that the Indian people's role of dependence be replaced by a role of equal status, opportunity and responsibility, a role they can share with all other Canadians.

This proposal is recognition of the necessity made plain in a year's intensive discussions with Indian people throughout Canada.

The policies proposed recognize that the separate legal status of Indians and the policies which have flowed from it have kept the Indian people apart from and behind other Canadians.

Many Indians, both in isolated communities and in cities, suffer from poverty. The discrimination which affects the poor, Indian and non-Indian alike, when compounded with a legal status that sets the Indian apart, provides dangerously fertile ground for social and cultural discrimination.

In recent years there has been a rapid increase in the Indian population. A forceful and articulate Indian leadership has developed to express the aspirations and needs of the Indian community. Given the opportunity, the Indian people can realize an immense human and cultural potential that will enhance their own well-being, that of the regions where they live, and of Canada.

The government believes that the framework within which individual Indians and bands could achieve full participation requires:

1. *that the legislative and constitutional bases of discrimination be removed;*
2. *that there be positive recognition by everyone of the unique contribution of Indian culture to Canadian life;*
3. *that services come through the same channels and from the same government agencies for all Canadians;*
4. *that those who are furthest behind be helped most;*
5. *that lawful obligations be recognized;*
6. *that control of Indian lands be transferred to the Indian people.*

The Government would be prepared to take the following steps to create this framework:

1. *Propose to Parliament that the Indian Act be repealed and take such legislative steps as may be necessary to enable Indians to control Indian lands and to acquire title to them.*
2. *Propose to the governments of the provinces that they take over the same responsibility for Indians that they have for other citizens in their provinces. The take-over would be accompanied by the transfer to the provinces of federal funds normally provided for Indian programs, augmented as may be necessary.*
3. *Make substantial funds available for Indian economic development as an interim measure.*
4. *Wind up that part of the Department of Indian Affairs and Northern Development which deals with Indian Affairs. The residual responsibilities of the Federal Government for programs in the field of Indian affairs would be transferred to other appropriate federal departments.*

In addition, the Government will appoint a Commissioner to consult with the Indians and to study and recommend acceptable procedures for the adjudication of claims.

The new policy looks to a better future for all Indian people wherever they may be. The measures for implementation are straightforward. They require discussion, consultation and negotiation with the Indian people—individuals, bands and associations—and with provincial governments.

Success will depend upon the co-operation and assistance of the Indians and the provinces. The Government needs this co-operation and will respond when it is offered.

Immediately upon receiving the full document, Elgie reviewed it, discussed it with the other members of the Board of Home Missions, and obtained their authorization to reply in the name of that board. The letter agrees with the general thrust of the policy, but expresses reservations on some points, particularly the intention to shift responsibilities to the provinces. This also elicited vociferous objections from the Indians. I quote the entire letter, and the reply by Jean Chrétien:

* * *

July 4, 1969

Hon. Jean Chrétien,
Minister of Indian Affairs
and Northern Development,
Ottawa, Ontario

Dear Mr. Chrétien:

We are indeed grateful to you for providing us, so promptly, with a copy of "A statement of the Government of Canada on Indian Policy." We have studied it with considerable interest and appreciation and hope that after further study and consultation the Indians will find in the policy a new opportunity to work with all levels of government toward the realization of their hopes and rights.

Although we expect some real difficulties in the implementation of the policy, we are reassured by your reply to a question in the house (Hansard P. 10644), when you said,

> *This is a working document which was tabled so that it may be considered by the Indians and the federal as well as provincial governments.*
>
> *We intend to undertake long discussions with the people concerned so as to find the procedure most appropriate under the circumstances.*

As a "working document" we also welcome this statement of policy as evidence of the government's willingness to accept drastic changes in its policy and administration if these prove to be necessary to "create a framework within which all persons and groups can seek their own goals."

We share with the Indians their justifiable apprehensions and fears at the prospect of the transfer of responsibility to the provinces. At least some of the provinces, and most of the people of Canada, will need to demonstrate a greater awareness of and a more genuine concern for the need of Indian People, before the federal government can properly relinquish its responsibility. The Policy recognizes this when it says, "Success will depend upon the co-operation and assistance of the Indians and Provinces. The Government seeks this co-operation and will respond when it is offered." (Underlining ours) If this principle is adhered to, the process may well take much longer than the five years suggested in the Policy. Nevertheless, we think it is significant that the government is prepared to relinquish its control of Indians Affairs within that time if it proves to be possible. We see this as evidence of its serious intention rather than as a firm time-table.

In the matter of Treaty rights, we accept in good faith your assurance in the House (Hansard P. 10645)—"The government acknowleges the legal rights of the Indians and the rights derived from legal documents." It may prove much more difficult for the Indians to accept these assurances in the light of their present lack of confidence in the government. However, if steps are taken promptly to initiate the proposed review of the Treaties, in co-operation with Indians, even this lack of trust can be dispelled in time. We agree that if justice is to be achieved for the Indians and other Canadians a reassessment of treaties may be necessary, as suggested on page 11 of the policy:

> *Government and the Indian people must reach a common understanding of the future role of the treaties. Some provisions will be found to have been discharged; others will have continuing importance. Many of the provisions and practices of another century may be considered irrelevant in the light of a rapidly changing society, and still others may be ended by mutual agreement.*

The Indian people are now well able to speak for themselves. There is no longer any need for us to speak for them, even if we could. We can but urge that every effort be made now to work with the Indians at all levels of government, so that they will have a really effective voice in the implementation of mutually acceptable policies which will emerge from or be built upon the statement of policy which you have presented.

The interest and concern of The United Church of Canada are firmly rooted in the early work of the Methodist and Presbyterian churches and have grown with the years. More than thirty thousand Indian people consider themselves to be part of our church family. We earnestly hope our influence may be constructive and such as to encourage the Indian people in their search for self-expression and self-determination. We believe that this primary concern for the fulfillment of the Indians' hopes will engage us in a common purpose so challenging and so demanding that there will be no room among us for self-seeking or competition.

You, sir, and your government, have opened a door. We trust we may all find the courage to use it.

Yours sincerely,

(signatures of Harold M. Bailey
E. E. M. Joblin
Esther M. Highfield
O. R. Howard)

EEMJ: sm

* * *

MINISTER OF
INDIAN AFFAIRS AND
NORTHERN DEVELOPMENT

MINISTRE DES
AFFAIRES INDIENNES
ET DU NORD CANADIEN

Reverend E. E. M. Joblin,
Board of Home Missions,
The United Church of Canada,
85 St. Clair Avenue East,
Toronto 7, Ontario

Dear Reverend Joblin:

Thank you very much for your two letters of July 4, and especially for the one signed also by the Rev. H. M. Bailey, Miss Esther M. Highfield, and the Rev. O. R. Howard, commenting on the Statement of the Government of Canada on Indian Policy.

I appreciated this letter more than I can say. Of all those I have received since these policy proposals were first put forward, it shows the most careful thought and deepest understanding of what it is the Government is proposing for the Indian people of Canada. I appreciate your perceptive and cogent remarks, which also reveal your awareness of the difficulties to be faced if these proposals are to be translated into reality. As you forecast, they have been widely misunderstood by many of the Indian people, who greeted them with fear, resentment and bewilderment. Only close consultation and discussion can create understanding of what this offer of freedom and equality means to them, and I am ready to embark on this as soon as they indicate that they wish the talks to begin.

You quoted my remark, "Success will depend upon the co-operation and assistance of the Indians and the Provinces." I might have added that for success we also need the sympathetic understanding and support of people such as you and your colleagues.

The 200 copies of the statement which my Executive Assistant, John Rae, promised would be sent if possible have already gone out to you. It was a pleasure to send them, because your letter assures me without doubt that your influence will be constructive and that your organization will be of enormous assistance in encouraging the Indian people in their search for equality, self-determination and responsibility.

Thank you again.

Yours sincerely,

Jean Chrétien

* * *

As a result of this support and in appreciation of his years of service on the Indian Affairs Committee, the minister sent Elgie a signed photograph of himself and his wife Aline.

Commenting on Indian criticism of the new policy, Elgie reported to the board, “Whatever its merits or faults, it has at least roused Indian leaders to the need of a statement of their own; if necessary, a counter-proposal. In their struggle for life, self-determination, and dignity, we shall all share, even though the manner of our sharing may not be clear.” Then, referring to further criticism of the past methods of the church and their impact on Indian culture, he continued, “for the past we need forgiveness and reconciliation; for the present, trust and co-operation; for the future, confidence and dedication. The traffic over this bridge must be two-way traffic.”

XXXIII A Surprise Resignation

At the annual meeting of the Board of Home Missions in 1969 Elgie submitted his resignation, maintaining that a younger man was needed to carry the load in his portfolio. Most assumed he was retiring; his hair had whitened during the fourteen years he had been with the Board. He had no intention of retiring. He was only sixty-one. What was behind this decision?

The reason he stated was true enough. But he confided to us that, since the board was amalgamating with another to form the Board of Mission in Canada, he wanted them to have a freer hand in the reorganization which would probably involve eliminating some positions. And he longed to return to his roots, and give his last five years before retirement to some rural parish. Was he also giving some thought to Helen, who had endured many weeks of loneliness while he was on his tours each year? She had a keen sense of humour. Had she told him she would like to see more of him than at breakfast when he returned from Ottawa at 8 a.m. and was due in the office at 9:30?

The board persuaded him to stay on until December 31st, 1970. Meanwhile, he submitted his name to the Settlement Committee of the Toronto Conference of the United Church. This meant that he did not seek a "Call." All self-sustaining churches had the right to seek a minister of their choice. This left "Aid-receiving" charges at the mercy of the Settlement Committee in naming a minister, usually a young ordinand. The result was that he was posted to Coboconk, Ontario, where the presbytery had recently decreed that two charges with eight communities should be combined into one. It was hardly a case of being "put out to pasture."

Meanwhile the tributes poured in. At his official retirement, the minutes first recorded a resume of service to the church since his appointment to Cordova Mines in 1928, forty-one years earlier. Then followed a less formal statement:

> The report on the Indian Work in 1969 is a finished product. Elgie may have begun his connection with the Indian Work in 1932 as a student minister with everything to learn about the Indian people, but though he moved through the intermediate steps as teacher and principal who could teach them, it is obvious from his report that he is one of the men who has helped to build the "two-way bridge" of which he speaks.
>
> He feels himself privileged, and reminds us that we are obligated as well as privileged to share in the Indians' struggle for life, self-determination, and dignity. Had the Government of Canada learned something of his humility and dedication in dealing with the native peoples, the climate today might have been more conducive to understanding and brotherhood—perhaps it will be yet.
>
> The report reveals an amazing grasp of a multitude of the details of the work, but more important still, a knowledge of the people, both those served and those serving them.
>
> When he says to his fellow-workers that "the Board is fortunate indeed to have the services of such able and dedicated men," we reach back into history for the response "Et tu!", you too, Elgie. The Board and the Indian people say, "Thank you, God, for Elgie!"

Then there was the commendation of the governing body of the United Church, expressed in part by its secretary, Dr. Ernest Long, as follows:

> The General Council passed a resolution expressing its great appreciation to you for a lifetime of service to the Indian people of Canada and for the very particular con-

tribution you have made to the Board of Home Missions. . .

The Indians themselves found an able voice in Chief Judge Nelles Buchanan of Alberta:

> . . . I am quite loath to have you depart the service of the Board. I don't know that I sympathize with your suggestion that the portion of the Board's work which you've been handling calls for a younger person . . . In any event, I express to you my thanks for the contribution you have made to my own life. The materials that have come from your pen from time to time have been most helpful . . .

The many subcommittees on which he served are well represented by this letter from Canon Puxley of the Ecumenical Institute of Canada, of which Elgie was a past chairman and on which he still sat:

> . . . Many people still so covet your wisdom and interest in this place that they wanted you to continue . . . The Executive asked me to write of our appreciation for all you have given to, and done for, this place . . . It would take me even more than my usual six pages per letter to begin to express what I feel!

And here are examples from workers in the field:

> . . . How we appreciate the contribution you have made in the area of Indian work. The experience and concern which you have brought made a great difference . . . One of the things I have admired in you is your toleration of the variety of ministry and personality of people in this work. Sometimes the variety included genuine originality, and sometimes it included short-sighted and short-lived efforts. But through it all you seemed to keep your cool.

> . . . Here in Manitoba we have felt the full impact of your concern and leadership as you have shown the capacity to bridge the gap between the native Canadians and the white majority. I am sure that time will reveal the greatness of your leadership and the enduring qualities of your Christian concern . . .
>
> . . . I doubt whether you will ever "step down" in the affections of the Indian workers . . .

Whether he stepped down at all in his efforts to serve in the new work to which he felt called we shall soon see.

Finale

Theme: Still Serving

XXXIV Back to the Country

It was no wonder that the Coboconk charge was available. Who, except Elgie, would want such a demanding position? Two charges, previously independent, had to be coaxed into cooperation as one, and officials from both brought together to plan and work collaboratively. Television now pre-empted Sunday evening, and yet time had to be found for four services. So on this "day of rest," he had services at 9, 10, and 11 a.m. and 2 p.m. To make this timetable possible, local elders would open or close a local service, while Elgie "drove like Jehu" in between them, in all seasons. Coboconk, Baddow, Kinmount, Norland—did he ever get the sequence mixed up? Then Burnt River, whose folk, like those of the other "closed" churches, were supposed to unite with one of these four, decided it wanted something of its own. Spearheaded by a group of young people, they settled for a mid-week meeting. The editor of the *United Church Observer* was impressed by all this, and wrote an account of the "man from headquarters" who gave up the job of an associate secretary to take on such an "aid receiving" pastorate.

But he enjoyed it. The congregation in Coboconk was made up, not only of villagers, but in summer of cottagers, some of whom, like Dr. William Service, he had known in Toronto. The other churches were supported largely by farming communities, and these were Elgie's kind of people "from away back." He made many close friends among them—friends who kept in close touch in the years that followed.

XXXV "Man Proposes, but God Disposes"

"In the years that followed"—what? A massive heart attack after three years of this kind of life. He had hoped to spend five years there, and the results of his visitations, meetings, and preaching were most encouraging. It became a self-supporting congregation, things were going well, Helen was busy in the women's organizations. After a lengthy stay in Lindsay Hospital, he tried again, but recurring angina gave a sharp warning. How embarrassing if he were to succumb in the pulpit! He resigned with genuine regret.

He wanted to be near enough to these good people to be at hand when needed, but far enough not to be in the way of his successor. In a new subdivision of Lindsay he bought a "pre-fab" with brick facing. Helen made the inside comfortable. With what strength he had, he improved the raw grounds, which included a cedar grove at the back through which ran a long-disused railway right of way. He found his strength returning.

In August of that year, 1974, they were able to attend the funeral of sister Gladys in Port Perry who had died of cancer after a courageous struggle. The brothers, Fred and myself, and sister Dorothy, insisted that they take home Gladys' colour television—the first they had. It gave Elgie and Helen much satisfaction during recuperation time.

"To be near . . . when needed": and he was, soon enough. His successor, Mr. Hudson, had just come from England—but his credentials had not. So in July and August, Elgie presided at four weddings. When Mr. Hudson could not always work in Burnt River, he asked his predecessor to do this also. Then in September, Lindsay Presbytery appointed him supervising pastor of the Janetville charge. This was required because Ted Power was still a student. The records show fairly frequent visits there for baptisms, communion services, and meetings of the official board. He was personally interested in Janetville because his father's first cousin, Leonard Joblin, had spent his life in that community and had been the choir leader in the church. He continued in this responsibility for three years.

A willing worker usually gets work. The presbytery also asked him to be their contact with the retired ministers and/or wives and widows. As he visited them he found that they were eager for more involvement with each other. To solve this problem, he established a yearly "get-together for fun and fellowship." This seemed to fill such a need that he built up a fund from his pension cheques that was sufficient to guarantee its continuation after his death.

Happily, this routine went on for some time, with requests here and there to take special services like anniversaries. These included returns to all five of the Coboconk churches, and forays farther afield such as the Seagrave charge where Dad had been minister during World War I, and to the Curve Lake Indian Reserve where Elgie had served forty-five years previously.

Suddenly the routine was shattered, this time by a blow to Helen. She had made an excellent recovery from the operation many years before. In February of 1977 she experienced great difficulty breathing. It got worse: the doctor ordered an ambulance. At the hospital they diagnosed heart failure, and drew an immense amount of fluid from her lungs. She was in the hospital for a month.

They did not want Elgie underfoot all the time, so he began cataloguing his extensive library of books and pamphlets on the Indians of North America. He realized that they might have to move to smaller quarters, so he sent the list to the United Church archivist, the Rev. Glen Lucas. Mr. Lucas came down from Toronto and returned with the first lot of cartons. Most of the material, much of it from the United States, was now out of print. Later he returned with his assistant and took back five more cartons of books and some files of information. They returned twice more as Elgie got his collected materials in order. All this included a good deal of material that I have used in writing this story:

2 large black binders on his field trips and reports
1 on the minutes of the Board of Home Missions on
  Indian work
1 on the history of the Mt. Elgin Institute
3 of *School News* that he had prepared for the Caradoc
  School District

2 of *Wampum*
2 of *The Manual for Indian Workers*
1 collection of articles by E. E. M. Joblin
1 annual report of the Department of Indian Affairs

All this was finished by November of 1979, when I took the last of it to the church archive. In addition, the archives of Trent University, Peterborough, which has a programme in aboriginal studies, accepted three cartons of material on Indian life past and present that was not related to his work for the church. Altogether these materials represented a lifetime of work and study.

Helen recovered; they bought a portable washing machine for the kitchen so she would not have to climb the basement stairs. Then it was Elgie's turn. In mid-March he blacked out and hit his head from the fall. "Only out 2 or 3 minutes," he noted in his journal. His doctor was concerned. Tests at the hospital showed that the heart had deteriorated, so pills were prescribed in addition to the nitroglycerin for the angina attacks. By April 10th, he reported "No problems; a good night's rest." After a quiet summer he began his seventh year of visiting the church pensioners.

"A visit from a friend is better than a vitamin pill." So he wrote when recounting the increasing number of visits from friends concerned for both of them. Besides members of the family, there were two sets of visitors that particularly pleased him. Three sisters from the Antone family of the Oneida Reserve, whom he had taught there, celebrated a reunion. Then there were Charles and Elaine Kitney, who had returned from long service in Trinidad and were now retired in Cannington. "Charlie" had been best man at their wedding. The Kewleys were in a class by themselves, now retired in Peterborough after fourteen years in Newfoundland where Arthur had been the minister at Gower Street United Church in St. John's. They would be the constant standbys from now on.

In January of '80, after a month of a new kind of misery, the doctor confirmed a case of hiatus hernia. Since little could be done about it except a change of diet, he ignored it except when severe attacks compelled him to sit up in his armchair since he could not lie down. He was able, in June, to preach at anniversary services at Cordova where he had begun his ministry as a student fifty-two years before. He had come almost full circle.

Now that his outside activities were curtailed he spent the days at his desk. Two projects were "in the works": a history of the Five Oaks Conference of Indian Workers (he had written to a great many participants to get their comments) and a Joblin family history. This had been begun by sister Gladys. He had taken it on when she died, and in his systematic way he did a thorough job over the years. He got information from immediate family, and from cousins of whose existence I was unaware. A connection in Texas was delighted to extend their family circle. A gold mine of information came from a distant cousin in London, England. Robert Barrett, "4th cousin twice removed" was on the staff of the Royal College of Heralds, and while employed in tracing the family trees of others had been doing the same for the Joblins. When he came to Toronto on business, he found my name in the telephone book and we had a fine time exchanging information. Genealogies were not my thing, so I gave him Elgie's address. The result was a boon to Her Majesty's postal services in the form of letters, copies from parish registers, and finally a vast scroll that looked like an upside-down tree. One root went back to the reign of James I, and the other to Scandinavian invaders in the ninth century. To compensate for an aunt of Oliver Cromwell and a succession of Sir Robert Flemings there was the usual couple of illegitimacies. The English are a great mixture, and the Joblins were English.

XXXVI Changes

Early in 1984 it was obvious that the health of both partners was deteriorating. They were unable to attend Cambridge Street Church; twice the minister brought communion to them. It also became obvious that they could no longer maintain a house. They were fortunate in getting a nice apartment at 502 Park Terrace that Helen liked. Their house (to which they had become much attached) sold immediately. After the mortgage was paid off, $50,000 remained, which Elgie promptly presented to the United Church Mission and Service Fund. They had a gift plan that paid good interest until the death of the donor.

The move was made in June. By November, Helen's condition, which for a long time had been diagnosed as anemia, got much worse, and she was taken to the hospital for tests. They showed a growth in the colon, which called for an immediate operation. There was a cancer so "massive" that most of the bowels had to be removed, and she was fitted with a colostomy. (Anemia indeed!) This created quite a problem for Elgie. It had to be changed too often for the visiting nurse to handle. She showed him how to attend to it, and beginning in January he was on his own. What with this, at any time of day or night, a severe case of shingles that he never mentioned to Helen, and the attempt to prepare food she would eat, he lost thirty pounds by June 3rd. This is when she died. During this time family, friends, and the faithful Kewleys visited as often as possible, but it was Elgie she wanted to have with her. Though his career required him to be absent a good deal, he made up for it in retirement and in the last difficult months. It had been a long relationship, from the time he "fell in love" when working on the Smith farm until now—sixty years. *Semper fidelis.* He had never had another "girlfriend." In his diary for that day he wrote: "Death is not extinguishing the light; it is putting out the lamp because dawn has come."

XXXVII Closer Family Ties

Of course his many friends rallied round, trying to fill a gap that cannot be filled. One visit that gave him great satisfaction was that of their old next-door neighbours from the Oneida Reserve, the Antones. His twenty-one years at Muncey had not been forgotten, and he was as eager for news as they were to share it. And in a sense he rediscovered his own family. Over the years there had been many visits to Elgie and Helen by two generations of Joblins, as his albums show. But while Helen was alive, their orientation had usually been towards her family. We regarded this as natural; while we were growing up our visits had been mostly to Mother's family, the Elgies. Now Elgie began to take the initiative.

That summer he visited us at our cottage. There was plenty of reminiscing, but the thing he seemed to enjoy most was—of all things—our harmonica duets. We had both learned to play a little on other instruments, but now we returned to our adolescence when we had played harmonicas at things like church socials. He had brought along both the mouth organs and a list of what we had once played. The family was very tolerant of this, and it became a feature of later reunions. It is not easy to adjust to the lifestyle of others, and it worried him that we had so many visitors, though their presence gave great pleasure to my wife. I found this note of concern in his diary: "Pat and King clearly lack the health and energy they need to maintain the standard of entertaining and activity they have been used to. It will not be easy to accept this and to become less generous to their friends and relations."

The following Christmas we began a custom that has been preserved in subsequent years: a family celebration. Each family celebrated the Day its own way, with Elgie then and always at the Kewleys'. But soon afterwards we all converged, and particularly enjoyed the progress of the third generation. Elgie and Helen had been denied the joy of children of their own. The close relation with the Kewleys had helped compensate. Now he found great pleasure in a whole parcel of nieces, nephews, and their offspring. The following summer he organized another kind of reunion, at brother Fred's cottage at the Gloucester Pool. The third generation enjoyed water sports; the other two mostly talked. Then he entertained the whole lot for dinner at the Rawley Lodge in Port Severn. This became an annual affair. Because Fred gave him meals at the cottage, Elgie insisted on paying for the food and in his will left a fund, the interest of which was to perpetuate this happy event. The children enjoyed the generosity of their great-uncle, and this celebration has kept his memory alive.

Mention of the fund brings to mind two substantial gifts he made after Helen's death. One endowed a nursing scholarship in her memory at Lindsay Hospital. The other was a $10,000 gift to his beloved "charge" of Coboconk. They had always lived frugally. Perhaps the habits begun at Muncey when they started at $900.00 a year stayed with them. They felt "passing rich" (to quote Oliver Goldsmith) in their retirement years, and what they did not need each month went into savings bonds. These were now cashed. It seems as if he was anticipating his own early demise, but the journal gives no hint of this. He was eager to honour the memory of the one who had stood by him "through all the changing scenes of life." The other gift pleased him because part of it went to maintain work at Burnt River in the event that it could not be served along with the other four appointments.

XXXVIII Keeping Track of Life

These gleanings from his journal call for a more thorough discussion of his lifelong habit of record keeping. The church regards his records as of real value. There had always been work with the Indians, but he was a pioneer in organizing it and carrying through new projects. Along with preparing all his material for the archives, he kept a daily diary from the time of his retirement. Most people make a stab at "Dear Diary," but he provides a full-size, page-a-day volume for each of sixteen years. It makes it possible to live his life with him, to share his delight at visits, his thoughts on meetings and political events, his pleasure at certain TV programmes when he was shut in. He expresses his frustration, too, when he must interrupt his work in order to rest. You feel his near-paralysis of will at the death of his wife, and sense his recovery as he resumes visiting pensioners and driving people to church or to shop, and taking part in local church and presbytery activities. Even when shut in, he was busy on the telephone, reminding people that they had not been forgotten. All sorts and conditions of humanity march across his pages.

In letters to his fellow workers in the old days he had included a page called "Flint and Steel," sparks of wisdom and humour that he picked out of his reading. Now in his diaries he ends each page with a quotable quotation. Where *did* they all come from? Here are a few of them: "Religion becomes not a stimulus but a sedative if it is used not as an inspiration to service but as a substitute for it." H. F. Fosdick. "What happens in worship? The holiness of God quickens the conscience; the truth of God feeds the mind; the beauty of God purges the imagination; the love of God opens the heart; the purpose of God subdues the will."—William Temple. "God often visits us, but we are not home."—Joseph Roux. "We make a living by what we get; a life by what we give . . ." "Worry is like a rocking chair. It will give you something to do, but it won't get you anywhere."—*The Observer*. "Man does not live by bread alone; he needs a little buttering up at times."—TV humourist.

What didn't get into the diary was a collection of cartoons he clipped from the *Observer*. I think he kept every one that the clever artist the Rev. Lawrence Purdy had drawn for that paper.

XXXIX An Honour Well-Deserved

Little space is given in that diary to an event that must have meant much to him; it certainly did to his family and friends. Victoria University conferred on him the honourary degree of Doctor of Divinity. He kept the citation given by Dr. Arthur Reynolds, the historian/archivist. It gives this overview of Elgie's life:

Elgie Ellingham Miller Joblin

> The Joblin family was not so much torn between the ministry and teaching as they were devoted to both. In fact, it could be said that the Joblins had a triple emphasis: pastoral ministry, missionary venture, and education.
>
> Not to go further back, Elgie Joblin's grandfather was active in the education of Indians at Red Deer, Alberta. His father spent his life's work as a teacher and a rural pastor. In his early years he undertook a mission to the Crees at Norway House and Cross Lake in northern Manitoba, and he ended his ministry at an Indian Church on Scugog Island.
>
> It is little wonder that a mission to the Indians got into Elgie Joblin's system at an early age. He had been molded by a family tradition; behind the family tradition lay the enthusiasm of Methodism in its concern for the Indian people of Canada.
>
> Elgie Joblin was accepted as a candidate for the ministry at the age of 19, and began his ministry at Cordova Mines near Peterborough. He entered Victoria College in 1930; and during a period of about five years, while at College, he shared in the work of ministry at the Curve Lake Indian Reserve near Peterborough.
>
> Graduating from Emmanuel College in 1936 with first class honours, he was ordained, and not long after

was married to Helen Smith, whose life has been dedicated to a dedicated man. At this time he was appointed to the Caradoc Mission at Muncey, in Middlesex Presbytery, one of the first missions to the Indians to be founded in Ontario. Within a few years a new church was needed, and with characteristic determination he directed the building of a modern church with facilities for community activities. It was a superior kind of church but Mr. Joblin had to raise the finances largely by his own ingenuity. The Board of Home Missions gladly supplied a generous grant, but a fair amount of the cost came out of Joblin pockets.

But something more than a Church was needed. Joblin found that the Canadian Indians were receiving an inferior education. But when he went to Ottawa to pry some money from the Government for school purposes, his request was rejected because he had no training in education and in the view of the authorities he shouldn't have been undertaking such a project at all. He then proceeded in his matter of fact way to supply himself with an M.A. in education at the University of Toronto at a considerable sacrifice. His thesis was published by the Department of Educational Research; and as a result he was nominated by the Board of Home Missions to the Indian Affairs Branch of the Federal Government and was appointed to undertake the educational work at Muncey and to implement recommendations made through his own study of the needs of the Indian people.

As a result of this move there came financial resources from the Federal Government which enabled Supervising Principal Joblin to employ a larger number of teachers, some in academic teaching, and others in craft and technical training. His understanding of the Indian and his expertise in education were such that the Hope Commission regarded the School as a model. Although he was the Principal, he taught in the classroom: and in baseball on the playing field he was both coach and umpire in the district league. He also initiated and directed other activities in the School, such as the development of musical talents, the organization of brass bands, and the edition of a quarterly magazine for the exchange of information and new ideas among those in charge of Indian missions.

In 1957 Mr. Joblin accepted an appointment as Assistant Secretary of the Board of Home Missions for Indian Work in The United Church of Canada. This entailed for him a new function in which he would be required to travel a great deal by train, car, plane, dog-team, motor-driven sled and by foot. As time went by he found that he was inevitably being pulled into a higher level of administration. One of his major concerns came to be the bringing of Presbyteries, wherever possible, into relationship with the mission to the Indians and with the Indians themselves. The aim, therefore, was decentralization, to move responsibilities for Indian work out of Toronto to the Presbyteries of the Church, and a fair number of Presbyteries proved to be very effective indeed. And while this was going on Mr. Joblin had to be in close touch with the authorities in Ottawa where major decisions were made with respect to the well-being of the Canadian Indians.

In 1970, Mr. Joblin resigned from the Board and accepted a pastoral charge at Coboconk, Ontario, where he has ministered for three years.

Elgie Joblin has not been subject to the glare of publicity, but we know how faithfully he has served Christ and his Church and the Indian of Canada. For 46 years he has carried on a dedicated ministry. It's a great thing when a person discovers what his work is, and the five members of the Joblin family knew clearly what they wanted to do. The two daughters became teachers, and elders of the Church. The three sons became ministers. Two of them already have the degree of Doctor of

Divinity, and one of them said: “You have kept the best wine until now.”

Quibus de causis, praeclarissime cancellari, praesento tibi Elgie Ellingham Miller Joblin, postulans ut eum admittas in gradum doctoris in divinitate, honoris causa.

XL Still Available: 1990-91

When he was forced to retire because of heart problems, I noted that he settled in Lindsay partly in order to be of continuing assistance to the Coboconk charge if their minister asked for help or if there were times when a minister was absent. Over the years he was happy to help when asked. When the minister was away in 1990, he received this letter expressing appreciation for such help:

> On behalf of Maurice, Norval, Harold, Evelyn and myself I wish to say "Thank you very much" for your help. As long as you live we will be coming to you for guidance. You have been so good to us up here and we appreciate you for your kindness and willingness.

He was also willing to be of service at Cambridge St. United Church whenever asked. Again, he was appreciated. He was grateful for that, and kept this card:

> We the members of your 1990-91 Bible Study Group want you to know that we sincerely appreciate your leadership. Your years of experience in His service, your knowledge of the Scriptures, your collection of clippings from various sources, and your very caring personality have helped us to grow in our faith in Christ Jesus.
>
> The signatures of each member follow.

That leadership must have been effective. There is proof of this in a little "Statement of Faith" by one of the men in the group. Apparently at the end of a series of studies he gave each member a blank card with the heading "The Gospel (Good News) according to . . ." No wonder he kept this one by D. M.:

> Because Jesus lives, we can live. Because the Holy Spirit enables us to believe Jesus, we have hope for

today and tomorrow and eternity. Because the Holy Spirit enables us, we can share God's love actively every moment. Because we can share the love and compassion of the Heavenly Parent, we will receive the joy of the Lord. Because of the God-love of Jesus, or the God-love lived by Jesus, we can follow that example by encouraging, forgiving, guiding, trusting, loving.

God can free all kinds of prisoners through us. We can be instruments of his peace, justice, and action. We can trust God and receive wisdom. We can be his people and he will be our God.

God, through Christ, is our Way, our Truth, and our Life. Therefore let us choose life!

There would surely be "joy in heaven" over such a testimony. There would certainly be joy for the leader of a group who could elicit such a response.

During his years of retirement in Lindsay, Elgie enjoyed good relations with the ministers of Cambridge Street Church. With the last one that relationship became so warm and friendly that it gave him great satisfaction. The Rev. Ruggles Constant arrived in 1991. From his first Sunday Elgie's comments in his diary were enthusiastic not only about the sermons, but also about the atmosphere of the Sunday social hour that followed, as each person experienced the evident interest of the new minister in him or her.

The personal bond began when he asked Elgie to have lunch with him. When Elgie recorded the invitation in his diary it was followed by an exclamation mark. It turned out that the new minister knew a good deal about his elderly parishioner—he had known his two nephews, Doug and Fred, at Victoria and Emmanuel Colleges. They met for lunch every month, and soon Ruggles was using him in the Children's Time in the service to talk about his adventures with the Indians. He became "Uncle Elgie" to them, and the new "uncle" was delighted.

It was a two-way relationship. In a letter to me after Elgie's death, Ruggles said, "He was a great friend, loyal and supportive, and I enjoyed his sense of humour. Though I was his pastor, in many ways he was mine. I found him extremely open to new ideas, and it was wonderful to have an older friend on the growing edge." Fortunate minister. Fortunate parishioner.

In December of 1991 there came an event that gave Elgie great satisfaction. He was invited back to Muncey for the fiftieth anniversary of the Oneida Church he had been instrumental in building, where he won the enthusiastic cooperation of the Indians and worked alongside them. The choir and local band had prominent parts in the service. What must have made him especially happy was that the minister was one of his former pupils who had gone on to ordination, the Rev. Grafton Antone. Finally, 142 years after Chief Peter Jones had founded the school in Muncey, his dream had come true: an Indian ministered to Indians there. Elgie had seen the beginning of this process in Muncey when he had helped Myrtle become a nurse, and in the intervening years he had taken particular notice of an aboriginal in any part of Canada who was providing leadership. In 1968 he was able to report that there were five ordained Indian United Church ministers and four candidates at college, one of whom, Stan McKay, was eventually to become moderator of the United Church.

At the end of his term in the church's highest position of leadership, Mr. McKay in 1988 joined the Dr. Jessie Saulteaux Resource Centre in Winnipeg as director. His title now is "Keeper of the Lodge." This centre is the successor to the Native Ministry Training Program. So far nineteen have been ordained, two commissioned, and two others are waiting for settlement, while seventeen students are currently studying full time. The dreams of Peter Jones, Elgie Joblin, and many others are being fulfilled.

The 1991 trip to Muncey was a kind of penultimate closing of the circle of his once-busy life of pastoral visitation. The last visitation, to which he drove his own car, took place on June 14th, 1992. He took part in the 125th anniversary of Wesley United Church on the charge that had included the Curve Lake Reserve where he had his first experience of ministering to Indians. It was sixty years after that formative period. "With long life will I satisfy him . . ."

XLI Winding Down

Early in 1992 Elgie realized that he would soon be unable to sustain an independent life. Shopping for food was taxing his strength. His rest periods were becoming more frequent. His eyesight was deteriorating, and he realized that it would eventually be unsafe to drive. But there was nothing wrong with his ability to plan and to act on his plans.

He was well acquainted with senior citizen institutions in town; his "pastoral visits" had made him familiar with them. He preferred "Caressent Care." He was shown a room there that would be available on June 1st, so he made the required deposit.

Now he set about divesting himself of possessions he could not take with him. Things that had a connection with Helen he took to her surviving relations. He was pleased to find that his nephew Fred had returned from his teaching job in California with his wife Kathie and baby Edward Elgie, and was settling in Parry Sound. They were as eager to have his furniture as he was to let them have it. They agreed on a reasonable price and on the date to move it.

Since they needed a more reliable car than the old Toyota station wagon that had brought them and their belongings across the continent, they were to get Elgie's car too for so much a month. This brought satisfaction to all concerned.

Measurements showed that he could take some essentials with him: his desk, a bookcase, and the metal cabinet with all his precious material on Indian work and family history. He was soon at that desk, uninterrupted by preparations for meals. He found the food there excellent. He entered into the life of the place, its "sing-alongs," and its Sunday afternoon worship led by local clergy.

For years he had been driving people to church, to hospitals, and for their shopping. Now it was his turn to be driven. He was happy to be picked up by old friends. It was a good opportunity for a chat. The minister and his wife even drove him to Toronto for my wife Pat's funeral in November.

Friends and family beat a path to his room. Their visits were eagerly anticipated; he was less of a recluse than ever. To make sure his more distant relations kept in touch, it became his habit to send Long

Distance certificates as a welcome hint. To some unfortunate people life in an "institution" is like going to prison. Yet there were no bars to his life except the limitations of his strength. One of the pages of his diary during this time ended with this quotation from William Blake:

> The bird, a nest;
> The spider, a web;
> The man, friendship.

He recalled a quotation from family prayers, now nearly eight decades before: "The lines have fallen to me in pleasant places" (Ps. 16:6).

Coda: An Analogy

XLII "I Have Fought the Good Fight, I Have Kept the Faith"

So wrote St. Paul as he neared the end. And so might Elgie have written, though his end came more peacefully than that of the doughty warrior for that Faith whom he greatly admired. On Thursday, November 18th, 1993, Dorothy and Henry had taken him out to lunch, as they had been doing frequently. After recording this and noting that he sent back with them Dad's handwritten diary for me, he finished the diary entry, "I am fighting to check a sore throat, which could lead to worse if not stopped. Will stay home tomorrow and see how it turns out."

It did not turn out well. When he was missed at dinner the next day, the matron went to his room and found him unconscious. The ambulance took him to the hospital that he knew so well. On Saturday I was called. When asked about his condition, they said he could take the call himself, he was just a bit breathless. I told him I couldn't get out until Monday; I had fallen that morning while collecting parcels for our church's food drive, and had to get new glasses. He replied, "Don't bother coming out; we can talk on the telephone anytime." He died that night.

I have observed that at the bottom of every page in his diary he put a quip or a wise saying. This was his last entry: "Some men storm imaginary Alps all their lives, and die in the foothills cursing difficulties that do not exist." -E. W. Howe. Elgie had climbed real mountains, though never at a height from which he could look at the view ahead with serenity.

Not long before his death, friends from Kinmount Church visited him and told him of plans for the future that might not be fulfilled for lack of funds. He told them that if they worked out a proposal that might fail for that lack, he would give $1,000.00. And when his will was read, he left everything (after his obligations) to the Mission and Service Fund of the United Church. This was no surprise to us. He had already told us his plans. We didn't need money; the work of the church did. It already had the $50,000.00 from the sale of his house. There is a biblical verse that says, "He being dead yet speaketh."

His friends from Lindsay and the five churches on the Coboconk charge filled Cambridge St. United for his funeral. The Rev. Ruggles Constant conducted it; his lifelong friend Dr. Arthur Kewley gave the eulogy. He began:

> We gather today to express sympathy to the family and close friends now bereaved; to appreciate the life of a faithful minister and friend; to celebrate with thanksgiving the contribution he made to his family, his church, and especially the native people; to proclaim the gospel of life and immortality in which he firmly believed, to which he was firmly committed and to which he gave faithful expression; to recognize the integrity, companionship and devotion, by which he stimulated many minds, conveyed visions of a new day, gave faith and courage to many. He was certainly an unsung hero of our church.

After reviewing that lifetime of service, he referred to their personal ties, not forgetting, I am glad to say, a tribute to the faithful Helen:

> For me, Elgie was close to being the brother I never had. We shared ideals, theological positions, missionary imperatives: the social events at our home with Elgie and Helen who were family favourites are happily remembered. Helen was an intimate friend of Fay. Her humour, intelligence, competence and charm enhanced our celebrations. None of our relatives held a higher place in the affection and happiness of our children than that wonderful Joblin pair . . .

He closed with these familiar words from Bunyan's *Pilgrim's Progress*:

> When the day came when he must go hence many accompanied him to the riverside, into which as he went he said, "O Death, where is thy sting?" And as he went deeper he said, "O Grave, where is thy victory?" So he passed over, and all the trumpets sounded for him on the other side.

For me, this quotation triggered a memory of a prayer in J. H. Oldham's *Devotional Diary*, a small book that both of us had used with great appreciation. At the conclusion of the page with the title "The Adventure of Faith" comes this prayer, which reminded me of Elgie's venture when he had sold all—including his cottage—to prepare himself for a new calling:

> O thou who art heroic life, keep alive in our hearts that adventurous spirit, which makes men scorn the way of safety, so that they will be done. For so only, O Lord, shall we be worthy of those courageous souls who in every age have ventured all in obedience to the call, and for whom the trumpets have sounded on the other side.

He was buried in Lindsay Cemetery, beside Helen in a plot overlooking the Scugog River. When he bought it was he thinking of its symbolism? The river empties into the Kawartha chain of lakes through which the Trent Canal system travels. So some of its water might wash the shore of Buckhorn, where he had built his beloved cottage; some would lap the Curve Lake Reserve; some pass the manse at Coboconk, thus linking most of his earliest and latest charges.

If you trace this river back to its sources, you come upon Lake Scugog, on whose banks sits the lovely village of Port Perry, where he had found a house in which his parents could retire. *That* lake was fed by the Nonquon River (really a creek) that ran through Seagrave. And *that* was where he had started school and where he had first answered the invitation "to all who love the Lord Jesus," to share in the fellowship of the committed.

I like this river symbolism for Elgie. A river goes places and accomplishes things. In many ways it keeps having an influence until it merges at last with the ocean. Elgie's influence continues in the lives he touched and in the changing attitudes to and treatment of our aboriginals. Between the Nonquon and Scugog Rivers there is a widening called Lake Scugog. The widening in Elgie's life was the thirty-nine years spent in serving his beloved "Indians." That service should not be forgotten.

Appendix I

It has been noted earlier that Elgie emphasized how Indian workers should keep in touch with one another and have helpful materials at hand lest they go "stale." Copies in the United Church Archives of *Wampum*, *School News*, *The Manual for Indian Workers*, and his *Quarterly Letters* show the effort he put into these materials.

If he were writing these letters in the last decade of the twentieth century instead of forty or fifty years earlier, their content would no doubt be different. Today there has been a rediscovery of native spirituality and its expressions through the burning of sweet grass, "cleansing" through the sweat lodge, chants, and healing circles. The use of these practices would no doubt be discussed, not dismissed. The last sentence of his Letter for June 1961, provides the clue to this: "Give the Indian the Gospel and let him create the native Indian Church." How happy he would be that, succeeding the annual study session at Five Oaks which he started, there are now two theological colleges for the training of native leaders, as well as the All Native Circle Conference governing the thirty-nine congregations led by native leaders.

The current situation is illustrated by a late 90's newspaper article stating that the United Church had dismissed a minister from his Indian congregation because he had introduced native ceremonies into his services. This was misleading, according to a reply from headquarters. Such ceremonies could be incorporated if the congregation wished them. The white minister imposed them against their wishes. This was in Southern Ontario; they had left these practices behind a century and a half before, and they were meaningless now. Apparently the basic problem was the personality of the preacher.

Appendix II

The following quotation is from one of Elgie's early reports to the Board of Home Missions:

It is no longer acceptable for one of <u>*us*</u> *to speak* <u>*for*</u> *the Indians, but rather to further opportunities for them to express themselves . . .*

Ecumenical co-operation should be the order of the day. In our witness to the Indians we have a terrible confusion to correct . . . The Christian Church is in danger of being completely repudiated. We are accused of taking away their gods and their religion. In the early days we gave them a God to worship whom they could understand and live and die for. That God was Jesus. In later years we offer our current god—money and what money will buy . . .

The dilemma facing the Indians is a desperate one—the old or the new, the Indian way or the white man's way, special status or equal status. At present their house is divided on the issue, and the final decision must be theirs. When more of them have worked out a synthesis of the best of the two cultures, and find the wisdom and courage to demand equal instead of special status, they will be able to look forward instead of backward. For them, as for anyone, "There must come a moment when all mirrors turn into windows."

> Let us not look backward in anger, or forward in fear,
> but around in awareness.
>
> – James Thurber

Appendix III

The Residential Schools (See also pp. 93, 103)

It will be evident that from the first Elgie was not an enthusiastic supporter of residential schools. He believed that young children, who often went away to school at age six, should remain in a home environment. Where this was made possible by the building of more and better day schools, following the pattern of his pilot project at Muncey, it was done. But often pupils came from areas where there were no schools, or where the schools did not go past Grade VI. For them he encouraged boarding in private homes near to their schools. Even where the residential school had a long tradition, this practice could be followed, thus eliminating crowded dormitories and providing more private space. His success in implementing this new policy (made possible, of course, by local cooperation), can be seen in the following statistic from his 1962 report:

> Our Church continued to operate, on behalf of the Government of Canada, six residential schools, as follows:

Norway House:	107 pupils in residence; 173 day pupils; all grades up to VIII.
Brandon:	156 pupils in residence; 90 in town schools up to Grade VI, 35 in private homes.
Portage La Prairie:	90 pupils in residence; all attend town schools; to Grade XII.
Edmonton:	111 pupils in residence; all attend town schools; to Grade XII.
Morley:	61 pupils in residence; 204 day pupils; to Grade IX.
Alberni:	247 pupils in residence; 111 attend town schools (VII to XII).

> Our church-owned residences at Teulon were continued, with 17 boys and 6 girls attending classes in the town schools. If there is a future for these residences it would seem to be in providing an educational opportunity for non-Treaty young people. In Prince Rupert, our residence for boys is in its second year and has its full quota of pupils (30). We share the concern of the government to keep up to the demand for classrooms and teachers for the rapid increase in school population. In spite of the large numbers attending integrated schools, it seems impossible to keep up with the demand.

Note Elgie's concern here for non-Treaty youth who did not receive the same attention as the others. At one point he got an interview with the minister of education in Manitoba, the province where the problem was most acute. He reported that the Hon. S. E. McLean was very cooperative.

The records show how faithfully he visited the six residential schools while on his tours of the reserves. But we have given no space to the reports he prepared to secure the board's action when it was necessary. Where the schools were well run, he was warm in his praise. Where they were not, he could be devastating in his criticism. This was the case for one of the six in his 1962 report:

Staff:	poorly led, poorly trained, poorly paid.
Food:	insufficient government allowance per pupil; badly prepared anyway.
Discipline:	no code of behaviour, no pupil participation in setting rules.

At the same school, he encountered the first wave of the serious criticism that was to emerge a couple of decades later. A "Study Group of Welfare Services" reported to the presbytery the occurrence of discipline problems and some student discontent. There was no mention of sexual misconduct. (This does not prove it was not there; in the recent court case in Alberni, B.C., where one man was responsible for the atrocities, the doctor who visited the school regularly testified that he had never heard of such irregularities in all the years he had served. The perpetrator, it is assumed, had "put the fear" into his victims.)

In this case, Elgie urged the study group not to be satisfied with leaving others to follow up, but to take the following actions:

1. Assist in the placement of pupils in private homes.
2. Find employment for students who graduated, and help them adjust to their new life.
3. Study wider problems of Indians in the area, especially the problem of unemployment.
4. Arrange for pupils to be entertained in churches and homes.
5. Make sure that pupils knew they were to report any injustices or ill-treatment to the principal.

Eventually the board closed that school after other arrangements had been made for the students.

In spite of his criticism, Elgie was well aware of the contribution made by the schools over the past century. He knew of large numbers of graduates who had "made good" because they had their start there. Even graduates who *were* critical often admitted this. An example was a recent moderator of the United Church who had his start in a Presbyterian residential school. And Elgie was delighted when three delegates sought him out at one of his early Indian conferences and told him they had attended the Red Deer School when his grandfather, John Joblin, had been assistant superintendent. They had nothing but praise for their treatment in their years there.

Nevertheless, recent years have brought a barrage of criticism aimed at many schools run by the denominations: Roman Catholic, Anglican, Presbyterian, and United Church.

Elgie would have been horrified at the stories of sexual abuse that began to emerge some time after his retirement, first at Mt. Cashel Catholic School, and then at others. But the growing outcry among aboriginals against the residential schools was not simply against such sexual abuse. After all, this had occurred in only a few schools. The main charge was against what we may call cultural genocide. In the attempt to obtain their assimilation, pupils had been forbidden to use their own languages and were punished for infractions. Long hair was cut. In some cases, even the drawing of animals was frowned upon lest they be connected with "pagan" rites. Perhaps if employment had been found for them after graduation the outcome might have been different, but they were usually sent back to their reserves, where they were strangers among their own people.

By 1969 all United Church residential schools had been shut down. In 1986, the moderator, Robert Smith, apologized to the aboriginals on behalf of the church. A "Healing Fund" was established, with the goal of raising two million dollars. A council of native elders distributed this money for crisis counselling, healing retreats, recovery of native traditions, education projects, and employment opportunities. In the *Toronto Star* for June 26th, 1999, a story with a four-column heading, "Church Funds Spiritual Healing," tells of one recipient who had been abused at a school (not United Church) whose life was turned around after years of alcoholism. When he had "hit bottom," a street worker sent him to a detox centre and then to Pendahbun Lodge in Toronto. A grant from the Healing Fund made it possible for him to launch a career in both Ojibwa and English. He has been able to combine his native traditions with his new Christian ones acquired as a member of the United Church in Guelph. "No one from the United Church is telling me what to do," he reports. The church has come a long way.

In 1999, the courts ruled that the government and the churches are responsible for damages received during the children's stay in the residential schools. But the main problem remains. A century and a half ago Chief Peter Jones foresaw the disappearance of the First Nations' hunting grounds, and took action to make it possible for their young to make their way in a new culture. Church and state agreed with him, and the Mt. Elgin Residential School at Muncey was the first response in Upper Canada. Sixty years ago Elgie saw the flaws in these schools as they had developed, as well as the contribution they made. His solution was adequate schools in each reserve, with well-trained teachers, teaching the history and culture of the aboriginals, making it possible for those with the desire and ability to qualify for successful integration, and training those who chose to remain on the reserve skills to make those reserves self-sustaining. He also demonstrated the viability of this solution, winning the consent of the church and of the government that bears the responsibility for education at First Nations schools.

Appendix IV

The Organization of the United Church of Canada

The United Church was formed in 1925 by the union of the Congregationalists, the Methodists, and two thirds of the Presbyterians. It is a democratic church, led by a General Council that is composed of equal numbers of laypersons and ordained ministers. These are chosen by the conferences which meet annually and are associations of churches (or "charges") covering a large area. Their members, in turn, are of equal numbers of lay and ordained representatives of the presbyteries which are composed of small groups of local churches. There is a constitution called *The Manual*, whose rules can only be changed by the assent of the presbyteries.

The General Council elects a moderator for each three-year period. These have given outstanding leadership and represent a large cross-section of the church. Among them have been an aboriginal, several laypersons including the popular medical missionary Robert McClure, several women, and the beloved black Wilbur Howard.

The wide work of the church is controlled by seven "divisions" composed of elected members who advise their "secretaries." One of these, Mission in Canada, now subsumes the Board of Home Missions under whom Elgie served all his life. One other term used here is the *manse*, the home of the minister, and which corresponds to such terms as "parsonage" and "rectory."

Appendix V

In 1960 and 1962 Elgie was asked to investigate the situation in Northern Manitoba. Charges had been made in the Toronto press that the Indians were starving because INCO would not hire Indians. This is his report:

* * *

Problems Facing the Indians

As human history is measured, the period of time since the Indians of northern Canada depended almost entirely on fish and game is very short. It was an uncertain, nomadic existence with much hardship at times. Nevertheless, the family was a close-knit unit in which the responsibilities of the parents were clearly defined and included the training of the children. The relatively small units of population were free to follow the game and adapt themselves to the changing seasons. With the coming of the Europeans, the Indians quickly learned to use guns and steel traps to increase their catch of fur for the trader. But the change made him more or less dependent on the trade goods of the white man, his movements were not quite so free, his "wealth" was more than ever based upon the uncertainties of the trap line. It was a trading economy which depended on his credit at the trading post. The value received for his furs was more and more dependent upon world markets, the demand for furs and the higher costs of the trade goods. It became a bad case of diminishing returns.

In recent years, a more serious adjustment has been required of these people. For nearly 100 years, most children who received any formal schooling had to leave home and live in one of the residential schools. With the increase in population (the highest rate in Canada), and in order to provide educational opportunities for all the children, the Indian Affairs Branch has been building up the Day School system on the reserves. The facilities and personnel have been remarkably improved since 1945. But this makes it necessary for the family to remain in a community for the school year. In order to continue to trap and fish, the father must go off by himself, or with his older sons, for long periods of time, leaving the family to manage without him. But it is more difficult for him to manage without them, since the care of the fur was usually the work of the women. With the new emphasis on regular school attendance which is the condition for receiving the Family Allowances, and with the increase in several types of social welfare payments and pensions, it is not to be wondered at if many men are inclined to remain at home with their families. They sacrifice their own independence and self-respect in order to give their children a chance. The price is too high.

The Indian has many problems, not least of which is to understand his white brothers. We introduce a cash economy without providing ways to earn wages and then complain when the men seem satisfied to accept relief. We insist on a white man's education for their children, but fail to provide opportunities for employment which would enable them to adopt our way of life if they wish to do so. We legalize and advertise liquor, and throw them in jail if they get drunk. We preach brotherhood and sharing, which they can understand, but we ourselves practise private ownership and competition in business matters. We build a church costing as much as all the Indian homes in the community and ask them to supply the fuel. We tell them about one God and Father of all men, yet we do not agree among ourselves. Truly, we are a strange, unpredictable, inconsistent people, with very little real understanding of his inner feelings, and little inclination to meet him part way in the process of adjustment. We are annoyed with him when he charters a plane to bring out his catch of furs, reducing the amount he can spend on his family, but getting home to them several days sooner. We cannot understand the fleeting sense of prestige this gives him, or the simple logic which justifies it. Truly, we are a big part of his problem.

He has problems within himself, which are common to most people. He has not yet learned to choose wisely between necessities and luxuries, to postpone a present pleasure for something more important in the future. He has not yet had time to acquire a true set of values, surrounded as he is with such a bewildering array of attractive things which are really beyond his means. Too much money is thrown away on bingo games, home brew, soft drinks, movies and alcohol. Many could live quite well on the income they have if they used it for necessities. Or so it appears to us. Who is to say what are necessities for them? These things they must work out for themselves as anyone else must do. Unfortunately, the learning process is often delayed by too much assistance from outside, and made more difficult by the example set by our people, who live among them on a scale which is impossible for them to attain. If a man is industrious and his wife a good manager, so that they "do a little better" than their neighbours, they are then expected to share with the rest or run the risk of being called a white man. This transition from the old ways to ours will be a difficult one to make, whether on the reserve or in town, and will take many years. In the meantime there is very little incentive for an Indian family to raise its living standards above those of the community.

Problems Facing Employers

The recent publicity began with an attack on the International Nickel Company at Thompson, and this was followed by considerable pressure to compel them to recognize a "moral obligation" to employ people of Indian descent. This concentration on one company, when several others are also operating in the general area, was unfair. It was apparently felt that if they could break INCO down, they could then bring the smaller companies into line. But INCO has employed and now employs Indians. Officially, they cannot ask whether a man is Indian or Italian, but they insist, quite properly, that there must be no discrimination, either against or <u>in favour of</u> anyone on the basis of race or religion. That company or firm or employer or school which consistently adheres to this principle, which demands the same standards of work and conduct from all, regardless of race or creed, will in the long run serve our Indian people best. We should seek no favours for them, only a fair and equal opportunity with others. It is the responsibility of the Canadian people, all of us, to see to it that they receive the training necessary to enable them to meet the required standard for employment and for life in non-Indian communities. They must have *sufficient education to enable them to make a choice between their way and ours.*

In the early stages of clearing and construction work at Thompson, the company hired a considerable number of Indians, for work which was more or less familiar to them. Smaller numbers are employed now, but most of the communities tell of men who were taken on but remained only two weeks. The kind of work available now in mining towns requires that the Indian make himself over completely and become a white man, if he is to compete with others in industrial work. For many of them, this is too high a price. To work regular shifts week after week, to take orders from other men, to live apart from their families, to stay on one job however uninteresting for the sake of steady employment—these are things the employer has a right to expect from his employees in this kind of work, but to do them an Indian has to turn his back on most of the habits and principles by which he has lived. Some have done it successfully, more will follow, but we have no right to expect large numbers to do so immediately.

There are other kinds of work more suited to them—seasonal work in the bush, building roads and power projects, commercial fishing, etc. We err greatly if we think, as some seem to have done, that if only INCO would employ large numbers of Indians, the needs of our northern Indians would be met immediately. At best, the mines can employ only a small fraction of the labour force available. Indeed, in view of the problems involved in necessary social adjustment, some of us are most reluctant to see large numbers of the people flocking to such centres—yet. In some important respects they can have a more wholesome life in their own communities. In terms of employment we should aim at diversity, and at work opportunities to which the Indians can more readily adapt themselves. Let us not decide in advance what the Indians of any area must do, just because we suddenly get in a hurry.

Let us admit that industrial and commercial firms in the north will employ Indians as soon as they are willing and able to "deliver the goods." It is to their advantage to do so, rather than to depend upon itinerant labourers who cannot stand the climate or the isolation. The new road being built from Nelson House to Thompson now, will enable the people to work in Thompson in a variety of jobs, without necessarily giving up their homes and community—forty miles will not be too far to commute, at least weekly.

There are problems involved in employing Indians in this area. They can be solved by understanding and cooperation, but not by ignoring them. They will not be solved until the Indians, one by one, decide they want the new, rather frightening way of life badly enough to pay the required price. Only he can make that decision and discipline himself for the sake of some desired goal. With or without our help, the future of the Indians depends on what they themselves do with the opportunites offered to them. These are greater than is generally supposed, and they will increase as both governments apply themselves to the problem, and as a newly-formed organization of businessmen in the Winnipeg area accepts the challenge of employment for people of Indian descent.

Problems Facing Administrators

It is pretty well known that the responsibility for the education, health and general welfare of the Indians rests with the Dominion Government and is administered by the Department of Citizenship and Immigration (Indian Affairs Branch) and the Department of National Health and Welfare (Indian Health Services). Non-Treaty Indians, known in Manitoba as Metis, are the responsibility of the Provincial Government. Manitoba has now about 50,000 people of Indian descent, about evenly divided between Indians and Metis. Their rate of increase is said to be more than 5%. In recent years the Manitoba government has achieved a degree of cooperation with the Indian Affairs Branch in positive action in Indian Affairs which should be an example to other provinces. Such cooperation has been realized in matters of education in most of Canada, but in Manitoba there have been significant achievements as well in economic and community development. In both governments there are able and dedicated men and women who do not deserve the kind of criticism and abuse which is heaped upon them by an uninformed press, some politicians and a too-readily inflamed public. The administrators have problems too!

One of the most difficult, I am sure, is the one just referred to. People with a superficial view of the situation, who know nothing of the prob-

lems involved in putting theories into practice among Indians, undertake to tell everyone how things ought to be done. Officials, already frustrated because they have not been able to accomplish the things they would like to have done, cannot defend themselves without the risk of casting reflections on the people they want to help. A few of the false assumptions which appear in these "helpful suggestions" are as follows:

I. All Indians naturally want to be like us. This is the same conceit which our race has shown throughout the world.

II. If they are economically depressed it is because they are shiftless or because the government has been too paternalistic. There is no such easy explanation for so complicated a matter.

III. All that is necessary is that somebody do more or spend more. It is assumed that methods which work in our society will of necessity produce the same results in a totally different society.

IV. All reserves are bad, they must be abolished immediately. To do so now, all at once, would be as great an injustice as some of the things we have been trying to correct. For some years yet reserves will be necessary to provide the sense of belonging and security which they cannot find among us. They will leave the reserves when they see the possibility of a better life elsewhere. This has been well expressed by several recent statements by Indians.

Running through most of these "solutions" to the problem, is the antiquated attitude that we must decide what is good for the Indian, presumably because of our superior knowledge and experience. We have no such right today. No proposal is acceptable which will deny the Indians the right of self-determination, within the laws of our country. Under the Declaration of Human Rights they should have the same voice in determining their future as other peoples in the world.

Another dilemma facing Indian Superintendents is the matter of the amount of financial assistance which should be provided for people who have no means of earning a living, even on the subsistence level. Many Canadians tend to feel that by our prolonged paternalism we have reduced these people to a state of dependence and denied to the heads of families the right to provide for their own. Yet what can an administrator do when faced with a family of hungry children, who are without sufficient clothing or fuel? Even when he knows that the assistnance makes it easier for the father to remain at home and do nothing, can he deny the necessities of life to the family? Lacking constructive programmes of self-help, and in the face of Canada-wide unemployment, what else can he do but give help on behalf of the Canadian people? And yet he knows that if this method is continued the people may soon lose any desire to provide for themselves, just as many have done in our own society. Such problems have not been solved in our own centres of population. Have we any right to be critical of men who are caught in the web, and feel compelled to meet need where they see it?

The matter of education is much too big to be dealt with satisfactorily here. But education has its dilemmas too. Do you educate the young for life on the reserve or in our towns? Should their education be academic or practical? Should it be provided mainly on the reserve or away from it? Should it continue to be a responsibility of the Dominion government or should it be administered by the provinces like the education of all other groups in Canada? Should secondary school pupils be placed in hostels or in private boarding homes? In practice a great many methods are followed. It would probably be true to say that the governments' best efforts have gone into education in recent years. Certainly the Indian people themselves have at last accepted the fact that they need an education if they are to have any kind of chance in this new age. Indian Affairs officials have always had another situation to contend with, namely, the involvement of the Churches in Indian Education. While a fairly satisfactory method of cooperation has been worked out, there is little doubt that this situation creates many additional problems for the Education Division. Perhaps the most hopeful development is the extent to which the Indian Affairs Branch has been able to work out cooperative undertakings with the provinces and school boards to enable Indian children to attend non-Indian schools. Almost one-third of all Indian pupils now attend such integrated classes.

One other problem for administrators must be mentioned. Now that the Indians have a vote, they are likely to become a political football and subject to a new kind of exploitation. All kinds of proposals will be put forward, most of them impractical and some of them unjust. With the public aroused to "the deplorable condition" of the Indians, it will take a good deal of patience and wisdom to maintain a sane policy of administration and at the same time to take advantage of any sound guidance which may be forthcoming. The wonder is that so many men and women of undoubted ability and high purpose remain in the Indian service. All kinds of people are climbing on the "Indian" bandwagon now. Fortunately, there are many very able and deeply concerned people among them, so that we have reason to hope that together the ultimate good of the Indian people will be achieved. Among many volunteer organizations involved, I should mention one which promises to be a valuable means of co-ordinating the efforts of the others. I refer to the Indian-Eskimo Association of Canada, with headquarters at 47 Dundonald Street, Toronto.

* * *

The wisdom and balance of this review are evidence also of his contribution to the committee on which he served the Department of Indian Affairs for many years, and justifies the praise of its secretary, Jean Chrétien, in 1969:

> I appreciated this letter more than I can say. Of all those I have received since these policy proposals were first put forward, it shows the most careful thought and deepest understanding of what it is the Government is proposing for the Indian people of Canada. I appreciate your perceptive and cogent remarks . . .

About the Author

Kingsley Joblin grew up in the town of Stirling, Ontario, where his father was a Methodist minister in the rural area around the town. At the age of sixteen Kingsley drove his father to the various services and meetings of his charge in a Model-T Ford. In doing so, he saw the vital role that Christian faith played in the lives of individuals, families, and communities. Gradually, he felt a sense of "call" to such a ministry. He enrolled in Victoria College in the fall of 1929, graduating from Emmanuel College in 1936. During the summers, he served on what then were called "mission fields" in Alberta, Saskatchewan, and Cockburn Island in Lake Huron. After four years as assistant minister at Deer Park United Church in Toronto, he became minister at Westminster United Church in Weston. This was to be his only pastoral charge. In 1946, he returned to the academic life on the staff of Victoria University, most of the time as Chairman of Religious Studies and Chaplain in Victoria College. Since his retirement in 1977 he has lived in Toronto indulging in his two favourite pastimes, reading and writing, and remaining active at Deer Park Church. This February he celebrated his 90th birthday.